Wine: Celebration and Ceremony

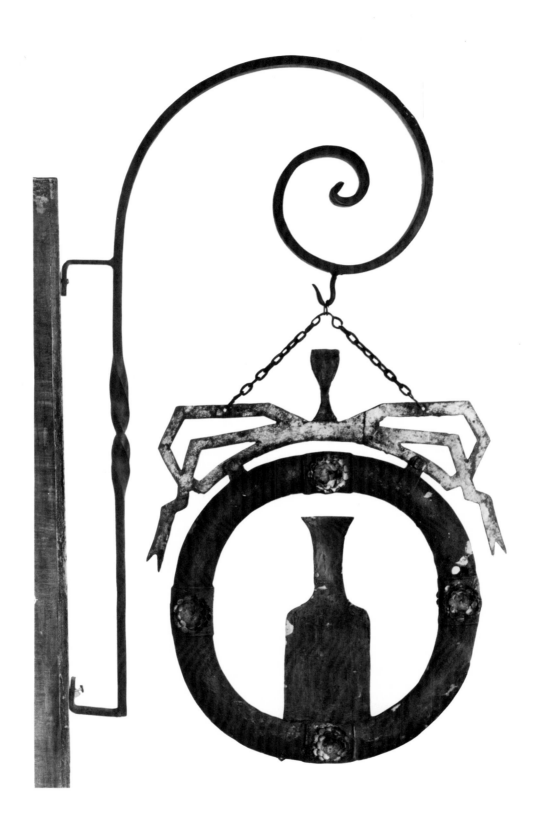

Wine: Celebration and Ceremony

Hugh Johnson
Dora Jane Janson
David Revere McFadden

Cooper-Hewitt Museum
The Smithsonian Institution's National Museum of Design
New York

Cover

Binding

For John Addington Symonds, ed. and trans., *Wine, Women and Song*, London: Chatto and Windus, 1884
Binding by Sangorski and Sutcliffe
London, England
Leather, gold, and amethyst pastes, 16.5 × 10.2
Cooper-Hewitt Museum Library, New York. Gift of Dorothy M. Rogers and Katherine Epler

Frontispiece

Inn sign

Late 19th century
Thann, Alsace
Metal, 48 × 40.5
Musée National des Arts et Traditions Populaires, Paris

Note: All dimensions are in centimeters and, unless otherwise specified, are arranged as height by width by depth.

Cooper-Hewitt Museum
The Smithsonian Institution's
National Museum of Design
2 East 91st Street, New York, N.Y. 10128

LC 85-71150
ISBN 0-910503-48-6
Printed in the United States

Edited by Nancy Akre and Lory Frankel
Designed by Katy Homans with Eric Ceputis
Typeset by Trufont Typographers
Printed by Mercantile Printing Company, Inc.

Library of Congress Cataloging in Publication Data
Johnson, Hugh
Wine, celebration and ceremony.

  Bibliography: p.
  1. Wine and wine making—History—Addresses, essays, lectures.
2. Drinking customs—History—Addresses, essays, lectures.
3. Wine in art—Addresses, lectures, essays
I. Janson, Dora Jane, 1916–
II. McFadden, David Revere
III. Cooper-Hewitt Museum.
TP549.W56 1985 641.2'2'07401471 85-71150
ISBN 0-910503-48-6

Photo Credits

M. Beaudenom, 85 (left); Christie's, 94; Flavio Faganello, Trento, 80; Patrick Guérin, Epernay, 88 (top), 102–3; Scott Hyde, 34 (top), 35, 72 (top), 104 (top), 104–5 (bottom), 110 (bottom); John Littleton, 119 (bottom); David A. Loggie, 21, 62; Michael Marsland, 77 (bottom); O. E. Nelson, 48 (top); Edmund Osterland, 38 (bottom); Jeff Ploskonka, Smithsonian Institution, 76; William Sims, 99 (center right); Sotheby's, 74; Luca Vignelli, 115 (bottom); Carmel Wilson, 78.

Contents

Foreword

We are deluged daily with countless sights, sounds, and sensations that may obscure our perception and appreciation of our surroundings. Regrettably, this results in many insights missed and many pleasures not experienced. The Cooper-Hewitt Museum's mission is to heighten public awareness of the designed environment. The Museum does this best, perhaps, by focusing on familiar, everyday, and often overlooked objects and showing them in new and unexpected contexts.

Wine is one of the most basic of beverages. Historically, it connects us to ancient civilizations, geographically to distant parts of the globe, and spiritually to the myths and beliefs that form our culture. Few subjects have surpassed the grapevine and wine as sources of inspiration for artists and artisans over the world. For millenniums, they have been a pervasive influence on design – not only in decoration and ornament, but in the numerous implements used in the production, serving, and drinking of wine.

While there is no way of knowing if the grape grew in Eden, the "noble vine" has enjoyed an exceedingly long life, during which it has greatly enriched the vocabulary of design. With interest in wine on the increase worldwide, it seems an appropriate moment to examine its impact on our culture and on the history of design.

This publication, which explores the symbolic, sacred, and secular importance of wine from antiquity to the present, is an extension of the exhibition *Wine: Celebration and Ceremony*. Both were made possible through the generous support of Moët & Chandon Champagnes and Hennessy Cognacs. We are deeply grateful to the sponsors and to all who participated in this enjoyable undertaking.

Lisa Taylor
Director
Cooper-Hewitt Museum

Introduction

Zum Wein wolt wir laufen
(Let's Make a Run for the Wine)
c. 1542
Hans Sebald Beham (1500-1550)
Germany
Engraving, 4.5 × 3
Cooper-Hewitt Museum, New
York. Gift of Leo Wallerstein,
1950-131-38

The publication *Wine: Celebration and Ceremony* accompanies the exhibition of the same title, June 4 to October 13, 1985. Both the publication and the exhibition provide a panoramic view of the interwoven histories of wine, history, and the arts. Each essay in this publication examines the history of wine from a different perspective; together, they give a profile of the distinguished and complex story of the vine and grape.

The overview of the history of wine production and enjoyment contributed by Mr. Johnson serves as a time line of culture, while Mrs. Janson's study of the symbolic importance of wine and vine in widely varying places and times suggests the rich historical texture of culture and viticulture around the world. The last essay offers a glimpse of the history of wine-related design over the centuries. All three essays illuminate the changes that have occurred in the production, enjoyment, and ceremonial uses of wine over thousands of years; at the same time, they celebrate the continuity that is such an important aspect of wine's history.

The generous cooperation of colleagues, collectors, and experts in the field of wine have been essential to the preparation of *Wine: Celebration and Ceremony*, both publication and exhibition. To the many people, too numerous to mention individually, who share our interest in the history of wine and design, we wish to express our profound gratitude for the assistance and advice they have provided. We wish especially to thank Deborah Sampson Shinn, Research Assistant, and Diana Larsen, Intern, for their invaluable help throughout this project, Cordelia Rose, Registrar, for her enthusiastic coordination of all loans, and Dorothy Twining Globus, Exhibitions Coordinator, and Robin Parkinson, Designer, for their inspired and lively installation of the exhibition.

David Revere McFadden
Curator of Decorative Arts

Lucy A. Fellowes
Project Coordinator

A Gift of the Gods

Hugh Johnson

Man learned to reap before he learned to sow. He (or more probably she) picked the first vintage off a wild vine, brought the bunches to a settlement, and gave a name to this sweet juicy nourishment, long before recorded history. No one knows when, and no one knows where.

Nor can anyone say when grape juice first fermented, or by what accident woman (let us give her the credit) first tasted wine, fizzy and cloudy with fermentation; first felt its warmth and felt her spirits rise; first became drunk, perhaps, and pressed the delicious poison, as Eve pressed the apple, on her unreluctant mate.

Persian mythology provides us with a story. The great King Jamsheed (Dshemshid) had a store of grapes kept in jars for eating when the fruit was out of season. In one of the jars the grapes, probably overripe, started to ferment, losing their sweetness and giving off a strange smell.

The jar was accordingly labeled as poisonous. But one of the ladies of Jamsheed's court had reason to want to kill herself and took some of the "poison." Far from finishing her off, it cured her melancholy. She told the king, who tasted, approved, and introduced wine to his subjects.

The earliest known work of literature agrees in crediting wine to a woman. The Sumerian *Epic of Gilgamesh*, a narrative from about two thousand years before Christ, related how the hero, journeying in search of eternal life, visits the land of the sun, a paradise in which he finds a vineyard. In it, "grape-vine was trellised, good to behold." Its keeper was a divine being, a woman who dispensed the "noble and precious fluid" she made from the vineyard, and which conferred immortality – but not on poor Gilgamesh, who has to journey on.

In his travels he meets the Babylonian equivalent of Noah, who relates the story of the Flood familiar to us in the Book of Genesis. Noah has a number of counterparts in Mediterranean and Near Eastern mythology – enough to indicate that the Flood is a historical fact. It may, indeed, be the memory of the thawing of the last Ice Age, when the sea level rose disastrously for dwellers on low-lying coasts and islands.

Basque mythology has a hero by the name of Ano who arrived by ship, bringing the knowledge of agriculture, and specifically the vine.

One version of the Dionysus legend of the Greeks was his arrival from the sea, where he had been nursed by the nymph Ino. Ino, Ano, Dionysus, Noah . . . strange that almost all their names seem to play with the same two syllables. *Oinos* is Greek for wine.

Speculation can lead us anywhere. Five-hundred-year-old Noah built his ark and stocked it with every living creature. When the waters dried up, he landed on Mount Ararat – on the borders, today, of Turkey and the Soviet Union. He "began to be a husbandman, and he planted a vineyard: and he drank of the wine, and was drunken; and he was uncovered within his tent."

But where did he come from, this survivor? All we know is where he landed. And if there were Noah figures in many other cultures, there were many landings – all with the vine, and the knowledge of how to use it. What was the country of the vine where they all took ship to escape

Habit de Cabaretier,

A Paris, Chez N de L'armessin, Rüe St Iacques, a la Pôme d'Or,   Avec Priuil du Roy,

the flood? One wild speculation is that the drowned civilization of Atlantis was the original home of wine. Russia claims that recent submarine
exploration found monumental architecture on the seabed not far from
Madeira.

More soberly, the best we know of the earliest wine-making justifies
Genesis rather than any later speculation. Ararat is most likely. The wine
vine, *Vitis vinifera*, in its wild form known as *sylvestris* (of the woods), is
a native of the temperate belt that runs around the fortieth north parallel, edging further north in western Europe under the moderating cli-
matic influence of the Atlantic Ocean. To the east the fortieth parallel
crosses the Caspian Sea, near Baku, runs across Armenia and northern
Turkey, then through Greece. In Italy the zone of similar climate moves
north, in the shelter of the Apennines, then follows the south coast of
France, reaching its furthest northerly point in the Rhône Valley, at about
Tain-l'Hermitage, and on the west coast at Bordeaux.

The first wine, then, could have been made at any point along the
route of the wild grapevine. It is tempting to think that Magdalenian
man, the superb artist of the Lascaux caves in southwest France, knew
the joy of wine. But the cave-painters were hunters in the last of the ice
ages, in a land of reindeer, mammoth, and bison. There were no vines in
France before the thaw – and the flood. The evidence still points to the
soundness of the Book of Genesis: to the country west of the Caspian Sea
– Armenia, northern Persia, or eastern Turkey – as the birthplace of
wine.

Rhyton
In the form of a reclining stag
c. 15th–13th century B.C.
Anatolia, Hittite, Empire period
Silver, 18 × 17
Norbert Schimmel Collection,
New York

Ritual libation and drinking vessels are among the earliest of ceremonial objects associated with wine. The narrative band at the mouth of this rhyton depicts figures performing various ceremonial activities, including offering a libation before a deity.

In this case the early vintners' first customers would have been the inhabitants of Mesopotamia, the Sumerians of Kish, and the Chaldeans of Ur, who developed urban civilization in the rich alluvial land between the Rivers Tigris and Euphrates.

Certainly the Mesopotamians imported copper from the north. They may have imported wine. But before long they imported vines and planted them themselves. The likelihood is that the first cultivated vineyards appeared in northern Mesopotamia – the country that was later to be ruled by the discerning Jamsheed – in the fourth or third millennium before Christ, at about the same time, that is, as the rise of Egyptian civilization.

The grapevine was not native to the Nile Valley. Yet the earliest Egyptian records show it flourishing there in a high degree of cultivation. We can only surmise that the short distance between the Syrian coast and the Nile Delta, some three hundred miles, was no impediment to trade, and that vines were brought to Egypt from Mesopotamia, possibly via Ugarit (modern Latakia in Syria) or Byblos (north of Beirut in modern Lebanon). It is scarcely assuming too much to suppose, then, that by about 3000 B.C. vineyards were planted and wine made in the area of Mount Lebanon and probably in Israel, too, and, just as probably, across the hundred-mile straits on the island of Cyprus.

The significance of these apparent byways in history is more than at first appears. Cyprus still makes, in its syrupy Commandaria, a wine that may be an echo of the wines of ancient time. Gaza in Palestine was known through the Middle Ages and its wine even imported into France. And the Bekaa Valley below Mount Lebanon is still producing wine of startling quality today. Its Château Musar is the only truly fine wine by modern standards that comes from the region of the first vineyards.

As for Turkey, the land of the Hittites, whose golden drinking vessels are the earliest examples of precious craftsmanship in the service of wine, today the Turkish State Monopoly makes its best red wine, by the name

Copy of a wall painting
Showing a scene of the vintage
From the tomb of Ipuy
Dynasty XIX, reign of
Ramses II,
c. 1304–1237 B.C.
Thebes, Egypt
Copy painted by C. K. Wilkinson
Tempera, 45 × 65
The Metropolitan Museum of
Art, New York. Rogers Fund,
1930

Amphora
Two-handled jar
5th century B.C.
Attributed to the Niobid Painter
Athens, Greece, said to be from
Nola
Pottery, red-figured decoration,
height 47
The Metropolitan Museum of
Art, New York. Purchased by
Subscription, 1899

The narrative on this amphora
shows Dionysus, god of wine,
receiving a libation. The wine is
being poured from a pitcher into
a flat, shallow *phiale*, a drinking
and libation vessel in common
use in the ancient world.

Tetradrachm
148 B.C.
Thasos, Greece
Silver, diameter 3.2
National Numismatic Collections, National Museum of American History, Smithsonian Institution, Washington, D.C.

The coin carries the image of a youthful Dionysus, god of wine.

of Buzbag, in eastern Anatolia near Elazig, within fifty miles of the upper Euphrates, and only two hundred from the 17,000-foot-high Mount Ararat. An experimental red from Anatolian grapes was made by order of Kemal Ataturk in 1929. I had the good fortune to taste it in Bordeaux in 1982 and took it to be a St. Emilion of the famous 1929 Bordeaux vintage! The ancient vintners, we may conclude, labored under no natural disadvantages. The region where wine was first made could still make first-class wine. It is not nature but the Koran, or rather its interpretation, that stands between the Near East and its birthright.

If evidence of appreciation and discrimination is anything to go by, we should have no doubts about the quality of ancient wine. The rations for the dead in Egyptian tombs of as early as 3000 B.C. included wine. Moreover, it was contained in jars labeled with inscribed seals showing the vineyard, the maker, and sometimes the vintage. One obviously much appreciated vineyard was called "Praised be Horus who is in the front of Heaven." Appellation, presumably, contrôlée.

It is Egyptian frescoes that give us our first clear and unequivocal pictures of wine being made: the grapes being picked from carefully trained arbors, being piled in vats and trodden, being pressed in a framework of cloth, being poured into jars to ferment. There is little in Egyptian techniques of four thousand years ago to surprise us – or that is not still used, somewhere, even today.

Clearly, wine gave the ancient Egyptians the same sort of pleasure as it gives us. They portrayed immortals sitting at table under shady arbors of

Worldly and Otherworldly Drunkenness
Leaf from Shams al-Din Muhammad Hafiz, *Diwan*, folio 135 recto
c. 1526–27
Sultan-Muhammad
Iran, Safavid Dynasty, 16th century
Ink, color, and gold on paper, 28.9 × 17.8
Private collection

One of three of Sultan-Muhammad's miniatures for the *Diwan* (collected works) of Hafiz (c. 1326–1390), the great Persian mystical poet, this painting is inscribed: "The angel of mercy took the cup of reveling." The scene is an allegory in which ecstasy, or spiritual intoxication, can be achieved in union with the Divine.

View of Bingen on the Rhine
From Daniel Meisner, *Thesaurus Philo-Politicus*
1624–26
Frankfurt, Germany
Engraving, 10.2 × 15.2
The Seagram Museum, Waterloo, Ontario

The Rhine Valley was an early and important center for wine-making and trading. The wines of this district were shipped to distant ports by way of the Rhine River, shown flowing among the vineyards.

Relief
Showing a wineshop
Early 2nd century
Italy
Marble, 28.7 × 42.5
The Metropolitan Museum of Art, New York. Fletcher Fund, 1925

This relief shows the interior of a Roman wineshop; amphorae filled with wine are stacked upright against the rear wall of the shop. A wine merchant negotiates the sale or transportation of a container of wine.

vines. It was the drink of banquets, of the powerful and prosperous — and we may be sure that the peasant and captive drank (if they were lucky) beer.

Egypt developed close links with the Minoan civilization of Crete, and via Crete with Mycenaean Greece. It may be that the Greeks learned their wine-making from the Egyptians, or the Minoans, or possibly from Syria direct. Certainly in the era that Homer describes (about 1200 B.C.), when Mycenae did battle with Troy, the image of wine is commonplace. The sea is "wine-dark." Achilles' magnificent shield, so lovingly delineated, is decorated with a vineyard at harvest time.

During the great flowering of Greek influence, between the eighth and the fourth centuries B.C., the Greeks carried their unique political vision, like the later colonizers of North America, to the savage lands to the west. Greek city-states founded colonies at Naples (Neapolis), Syracuse (Syracusae), and Marseille (Massilia), northward at Byzantium, and also in the Crimea. No one doubts that the colonists took their vines with them. What nobody knows is whether they found wine already in place in what were to be the vineyards of Italy, France, and Thrace: whether the native inhabitants had already discovered what could be made of the native vines.

At the same time that Greece was populating the north shore of the Mediterranean with new cities, the Phoenicians, Semitic seafarers from Tyre and Sidon in what is now Lebanon, pushed further south and west, beyond the sphere of the Greeks, to found their Punic cities – Tripoli in what is now Libya and Carthage in Tunisia – and to occupy southern Spain as far west as Cadiz, and probably northward into Portugal.

Before the founding of the Roman Empire, therefore, the whole Mediterranean seacoast had been colonized by wine-makers. The Roman legions marched into a theater already festooned with vines.

What did wine mean to those early Mediterranean civilizations? There are hints in images and epics that from the start it was more than a mere beverage. To Gilgamesh it had been out of reach: the drink of the immortals. When mortals drank it their intoxication made them feel godlike. The idea of the libation, pouring wine upon the ground as a gift to the gods, is connected with the earliest religious ritual. The Jews used wine in their sacrificial ceremonies; it came to take the place of, and hence to symbolize, blood. The Greeks celebrated Dionysus as the god of living and growing things, as the source of movement of sap in plants and of emotions in people. The beneficent aspects of the god were counterbalanced by darker forces: in Dionysiac orgies the priestesses of the god went wild, raving hysterically, tearing animals, and even children, limb from limb.

The *Bacchae* of Euripides is the New Testament of Dionysus. Grandson of King Cadmus, born of his daughter Semele and Zeus himself, he comes, he says, from Asia, from Phoenicia (or Tyria). So indeed did wine: the god identifies himself with wine, and thus wine with the mystery of his inspiration and his rites.

At a more humdrum level, it was impossible not to regard wine as a food – for such it is – with spiritual properties. Life was very much less comfortable, disease more painful, and society no more carefree in early times. Almost all human societies have some form of intoxicant or narcotic to raise man above his daily fatigue and enlarge his horizons. Wine seemed to be – indeed, still does – a divine gift to smooth man's path. Whereas other alcoholic drinks are artificially contrived to be stronger or weaker, grape juice ferments naturally to produce a drink with about 10 percent alcohol by volume (occasionally as high as 15 or as low as 7). Ten percent is a gentle measure: ideal for gradual assimilation, ideal to accompany food.

Vendemmie
(Vintage)
Plate 27 from *Le Antiche
Lucerne Sepolcrali Figurate*
1704
Domenica de Rossi after Pietro
Santi Bartoli (c. 1635–1700)
Rome, Italy
Engraving, 34.5 × 23.3
Cooper-Hewitt Museum
Library, New York

This print shows a Roman oil
lamp ornamented with a vintage
scene. In the center, a large cask
of wine is being drawn by oxen,
while two harvesters carry clusters and baskets of grapes. Three
woven reed baskets filled with
grapes are seen in the foreground.

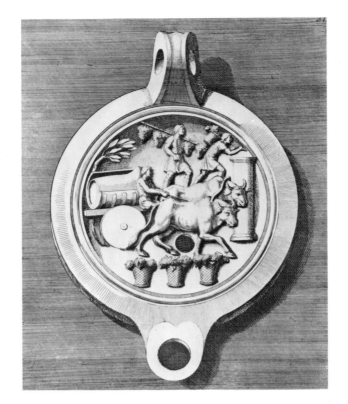

October
Leaf from a Flemish prayer
book, folio 11 verso
16th century
Simon Bening (1483–1561)
Flanders
Manuscript on vellum, 20 × 15
Courtesy Staatsbibliothek,
Munich

The painting shows wine merchants engaged in sampling recently arrived casks. While the
wine is being tasted from shallow bowls, workers are tapping
and refilling additional barrels.
In the background, a human
treadmill provides the power for
a crane that lifts filled casks to
and from the canal.

It is easy to see why Mediterranean cultures saw in wine a natural symbol for the spirit, and even confused the two. Christ's institution of the Sacrament was a logical progression from the already established meaning of bread and wine in Jewish custom.

What is far more difficult is to explain the rejection of wine by non-Mediterranean cultures. The Chinese have known it for many centuries, yet never took it into their diet. Even stranger, the followers of Islam, the direct descendants, it seems, of wine's discoverers, have outlawed it based upon their interpretation of the scriptures. This is not the place to debate the Koran, only to point out that prohibition is a late development of Islamic law.

Persian literature and art is full of references to wine-drinking, at least by those in authority. In the diaries of Sir John Chardin, the great jeweler who traveled with the court of Persia in the seventeenth century, we find as a centerpiece in the shah's sumptuous tent a vast golden wine cooler filled with flasks buried in snow from the mountains. Shiraz was famous for its grapevines.

The same association of wine and authority was common in ancient Rome. Of all the pleasures and privileges of power, none was rated more highly than the possession of a vineyard. The highest favor of the Roman Emperor Julian was the gift of a vineyard prepared – actually planted and pruned – by his own hands.

Subsequent parallels come readily to mind. Charlemagne is known to have planted vineyards and was said to have singled out the great south slope of Schloss Johannisberg. Abbots in the Middle Ages, courtiers in the Renaissance, Rothschilds in the nineteenth century held their vineyards as their proudest possessions.

It was the Romans who established all the great wine regions of what is now France. Gaul, according to Caesar's account, was at first a beer-drinking nation. Once they had tasted the wine of the Romans, though, the Gauls stopped at nothing to buy and drink to excess. One amphora of wine (twenty-six gallons) was reckoned fair barter for one slave. The trade in wine from Italy up the Rhône Valley, through Burgundy to Trier on the Moselle – the "northern Rome" that guarded the German frontiers – was at first a source of considerable wealth. Scarcely less so was the wine trade across southwest France, from the southern capital of Narbonne, via Gaillac and the Rivers Tarn and Garonne, to Bordeaux

Relief
Showing satyrs treading grapes
2nd–1st century B.C.
Campania, Italy, Graeco-Roman period
Terra-cotta, 33.8 × 43.5
Museum of Fine Arts, Boston.
Benjamine Pierce Cheney donation

Dressed in animal skins, the satyrs hold hands to steady themselves in the slippery treading vat; they work to the tune of pipe music provided by their animated young colleague.

Illumination
From Petrus de Crescentius,
*Livre des Profits Champestres et
Ruraux*, folio 77 recto
c. 1470
Master of Margaret of York
Bruges, Flanders
Manuscript on vellum,
42.1 × 32.4
The Pierpont Morgan Library,
New York. M. 232

This manuscript was probably
made for a member of the Bur-
gundian ducal family whose col-
ors are introduced on this page.
Outside the walls of a storeroom
for wine in casks, laborers are
pruning and harvesting the
vines. The treatise of Petrus de
Crescentius (Pietro de Crescenzi,
1230?–1320?) on rural life first
appeared in manuscript form in
about 1306, and continued to be
popular in printed form
through the end of the eighteenth century. The original version was in Latin, with later
editions translated into Italian,
French, German, and Polish.

and hence to the Celtic north — to Ireland in particular. Dredging opera-
tions at Chalon, the port on the River Saône where Italian wine was
transhipped for the overland journey to Trier (or via Autun to the Loire
and the west), have uncovered tens of thousands of broken amphorae.
We may assume that resident wine merchants invested their profits in
establishing vineyards around their entrepôt. The same assumption
would account for the planting of vines at Bordeaux.

But it runs counter to the strongly held Gallic view of Yves Forgeot, a
well-known historian of Burgundy. His version (supported by much evidence) is that the Celts from Burgundy made a highly successful incur-
sion into Italy two hundred years earlier. They occupied the Po Valley in
Lombardy, where they learned the cultivation of the vine, then went
home and set up shop, with unerring taste, on the Côte d'Or.

In each of the classic wine regions one is bound to stop and ask the
question, "Why here?" How did its planters know that Beaune, or
Champagne, or Graves, or St. Emilion would be a great wine-growing
area? Did they try every hillside? The answer is always more circumstan-
tial. Each "classic" vineyard of Roman foundation is either near a center
of population or an important trade route — preferably a river, for convenient transport. A cogent explanation of the development of Burgundy's
Côte d'Or is that it provided the *civitas*, or prefecture, of Autun with a
shopwindow on its boundary where the main road north ran from the
Saône to the Marne, Meuse, and Moselle. Autun, with no other vineyards of note, ploughed a fortune into the Côte d'Or and became celebrated as a result. There was never a great vineyard without great
investment, as we shall see.

Rome was not entirely happy about its subject Gaul planting vines
with such alacrity, nor with the undoubted fact that its wine was better
than that of Italy. Emperor Domitian (ruled A.D. 81-96) banned planting
and ordered half the vines of Gaul to be grubbed up. (Two hundred years

**Château du Clos de Vougeot and
vineyards in Burgundy**
c. 1950
Courtesy Conseil Régional de
Bourgogne, Dijon, France

ous auons dit plu
seurs choses des
plantes des vignes
par deuant quant
nous traittons de la comune
nature des plantes · Et a pre
sent en ce quart liure nous
voulons parler de la nature
et du labouraige des vignes
et de toutte maniere de vi
gnes · et de tout le prouffit

Du fruit en particulier·

De quel arbre est la vigne ·
de la vertu de ses fueilles · des
cendres ·

Chascun a cognoissance
des vignes que c'est
fort ce froides contrees ou le
fruit ne puet croistre · Si con
clud que c'est vn hamble ·plo
ant arbrillon moult tortu

later, Emperor Probus removed the interdict; it is hard to imagine it had ever been strictly imposed.)

Why was Gallic wine superior? Several elements must have contributed. Given sufficient money and motivation, there are four prime factors that decide the quality of wine: the grapevine, the soil, the weather, and the cellar conditions. These last are in turn determined by the possibility of underground cellars or caves and the prevailing climate from vintage time on into the winter. Steady cool temperatures are essential to ferment fine wine – as every California vintner knows.

The Gauls were fortunate with their grapevines. Perhaps they started with the Mediterranean vines brought by the Romans, or indeed the Levantine ones brought by the Greeks. (The Muscat may have been one of these.) But they soon started selecting and planting from among the native vines of southeastern France, the territory of the tribe of the Allobroges. Authorities from Pliny onward believe that from among the subalpine Allobrogian vines the great family of the Pinots appeared, to become the glory of Burgundy and Champagne.

Similarly, in Bordeaux by the end of the first century a vine known as the *Biturica* was well established (possibly, say some, from the wild vines of the Ebro Valley in Navarre). It is possible that this was the source of the Cabernet family.

In later Roman times the vine flourished farther north than it does today: along the Seine near Paris and into Normandy. In the vineyards of the Loire the traditions of Burgundy and Bordeaux, the Pinot and the Cabernet met, and still meet.

It is hard to overestimate the achievement of the Romans and their Gallic and German subjects. By the time the Empire declined and fell the foundations had been laid for all of what we consider the classic table wines. As the French historian Dion points out, immense pride and re-

Design for a Standing Cup with Cover
From the series *Novum Opus Cratero Graphicum . . .*
1551
Mathis Zündt (c. 1498–1572)
Nuremberg, Germany
Etching, 33.9 × 16.3
Cooper-Hewitt Museum, New York. Purchased in memory of Annie Schermerhorn Kane, 1944-82-2

spect for local practice develops rapidly, and it probably has as much effect in forming traditions as do physical conditions.

The distinctiveness of top quality wine is determined partly by soil, but surely it also emerges from a determination to cling to apparently significant local details. Study the Italian laws of Denominazione di Origine: each region makes a point of not doing the same as its neighbors. So (until wine-makers all started going to the same universities) it has gone on down the centuries.

Pleasure and prestige saved the vineyards (or some of them) after the Fall of Rome. A Vandal or a Visigothic king was no less susceptible to the appeal of a vineyard than his predecessors or his successors in power, the princes of the Church. An indication of the continuity of culture through centuries of strife lies in those Roman *civitates*, of which Autun was one. With very few exceptions they became the dioceses of bishoprics. Monasteries needed wine, both for their rites and to fulfill their role as the hotels of the Dark Ages.

Missionaries introduced more than religion in their travels. When Saint Colombanus set sail for Ireland from Nantes about A.D. 600 he took his Muscadet with him. Ireland continued to need a wine supply and shipped it from Brittany, the Seine, or England – wherever the sea passage was shortest. England in turn abandoned Bordeaux (where a "negotiator Britannicus" had been spotted in the first century) and landed wine from the Rhine and Rouen – not even via the Seine, for fear of Viking longships, but through a port at the mouth of the River Canche known as Quentovicus, until the marauding Norsemen burned it to the ground.

The slow renaissance of civilization in Europe did little to alter the legacy of Rome. The Vikings had demanded the wine of Reims as ransom – almost a thousand years before it was first called Champagne. Wine remained a symbol of power, enjoyed and exploited by princes for its unique properties, both as a source of pleasure and an object of trade.

What other goods were bulky and needed regular shipping? Grain was home-grown; precious articles were small and scarce; wool was a taxable commodity. Nothing took so much naval tonnage as wine, nor was harder to distribute undetected.

Monarchs (and later parliaments) learned to play cat-and-mouse with the wine trade. It was to be encouraged as a source of pleasure, health,

Wonderful Museum . . . :
"The Heidelberg Tun"
Published by R. S. Kirby and J.
Scott
1803
London, England
Engraving, 10.8 × 17.2
The Seagram Museum, Water-
loo, Ontario

The Heidelberg Tun, still located
in the cellar of Heidelberg Cas-
tle, was constructed in 1751 by
Jakob Engler the Younger. Made
for Elector Karl Theodor, it included a pump to bring wine to
the upper floor.

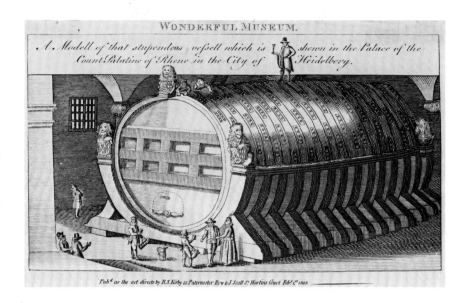

A Modell of that stupendous vessell which is shewn in the Palace of the Count Palatine of Rhene in the City of Heidelberg.

Habit de Tonnellier
(Costume of a Cooper)
c. 1690
Nicholas de Larmessin
(1640–1725)
Paris, France
Engraving, 32.5 × 23.5
Print Collection, The New York
Public Library, Astor, Lenox and
Tilden Foundations

Habit de Tonnellier

25

Flute glass
c. 1660
Possibly by C. F. Meyer
Holland or Flanders
Glass, height 39.4
Cinzano Collection (U.K.) Ltd.

This flute, which may have been
used for ale or wine, is engraved
with the arms of Charles II, and
was probably made to celebrate
the monarch's triumphant return
to the throne of England in 1660.

**Champagne Bottling at Pierry in
France**
From *The Illustrated London
News*, August, 1855
Engraving, 37 × 24.3
Cooper-Hewitt Museum Library,
New York. Kubler Collection

This engraving shows all of the
stages necessary in the bottling
of Champagne, including disgorging the sediment, inserting
the cork, fastening the cork with
string, sealing the cap of the bottle, and wrapping the bottle.

and profit (also as an incitement to build ships, and a means of training
sailors). At the same time it was to be milked for revenue through importation taxes, which encouraged smuggling. Smuggling has always been a
diverting subplot in its history – never more so than when in the early
eighteenth century, at the height of the French wars, England's first prime
minister, Sir Robert Walpole, then First Lord of the Admiralty, used his
State barge to bring his Bordeaux into King's Lynn harbor under the
noses of the excisemen.

Shakespeare provides moments of perfect focus on what London drank
in the sixteenth century. Bordeaux, after three centuries of English do-
minion, had been lost to the French. Nonetheless, the Falcon at South-
wark, the poet's "local," offered "old clarett," "Graves," and "Graves
clarret." The only other French wines on the list were Orliance (Orléans)
and Rochelle. Rhenish (or Rhine wine) was listed as "Deal," the port in
Kent at which it was landed. All the other wines on the list came into the
category of "Sack": heavy, more or less sweet and/or strong wines from
Mediterranean climates. Malligo, Sherry Sack, Malmsey, Alicante,
Moscadino, Arangossa, Canary, Charneco, Bastard, Peter-see-me (Pedro
Ximenez, from Spain), and Candy (from Candia, or Crete, later captured
by the Turks) were all cockle-warmers, popular as the strongest drink
before spirits appeared early in the next century, in the reign of King
James I. "If I had a thousand sons," says Falstaff, "the first humane
principle I would teach them should be, to forswear thin potations, and
to addict themselves to sack."

Up to Shakespeare's time, it is possible to argue, nothing substantive
had changed in the world of wine since the Roman Empire. It had remained a commodity of widely varying character, of high value, but still
relatively generic. What mattered was its strength and its age. The
stronger it was, the longer it would keep: light wines, kept in barrels,
"went off" so quickly that their price halved if they lasted into a second
year.

By the end of the seventeenth century one could say, as Molière did,
"Nous avons changé tout cela." First came competition from spirits and,
by the mid-seventeenth century, from coffee, chocolate, and tea. Second
came great advances in the manufacture of glass for bottles. Third (perhaps) came the cork.

A wine merchant's woes in the midcentury are summed up in the sad
little treatise called "The Mysterie of Vintners," one of the first papers
presented, in 1662, to the infant Royal Society in London. Its subtitle
tells it all: "A Brief Discourse concerning the various sicknesses of Wines,
and their respective Remedies, at this Day commonly used."

Hair-raising deathbed remedies, often involving large amounts of lead,
were the vintner's only recourse with wine that was subject to all manner
of ailments. It "pricked," turned "ropy," "fretted," "palled," and was
"invaded by unnatural and sickly commotions." The surest way of getting wine "piquant and gustful to the Palate, agreable to the Stomach,
and nutritive to the Body" was to drink it young, before it caught any
diseases.

The most important development in wine's long history was the unknown moment when cork came into use as the permanent stopper for
sufficiently well-made and uniform bottles. From being a mere carafe for
carrying wine from barrel to table, the bottle became, in essence, a mini-
barrel – and it was better than a barrel, because it did not leak or allow
evaporation.

We do not know who discovered that wine could keep indefinitely
when safely corked in a full bottle – or who first became aware that kept
in its bottle it changed slowly and subtly for the better. The first hard
evidence we have is a beautiful silver corkscrew, made in about 1680.
The corkscrew was a prerequisite for a firm and permanent cork.

Cellarers had known for centuries that wine in full barrels kept far

THE DISGORGER.   CORKING.   FASTENING THE CORK WITH STRING.

WRAPPING.   TINFOILING.   WIRING.   STRINGING.   CORKING.   DISGORGING.   PACKING.

FASTENING THE CORK WITH WIRE.   PUTTING ON THE TINFOIL.   WRAPPING THE BOTTLE IN PAPER.

27

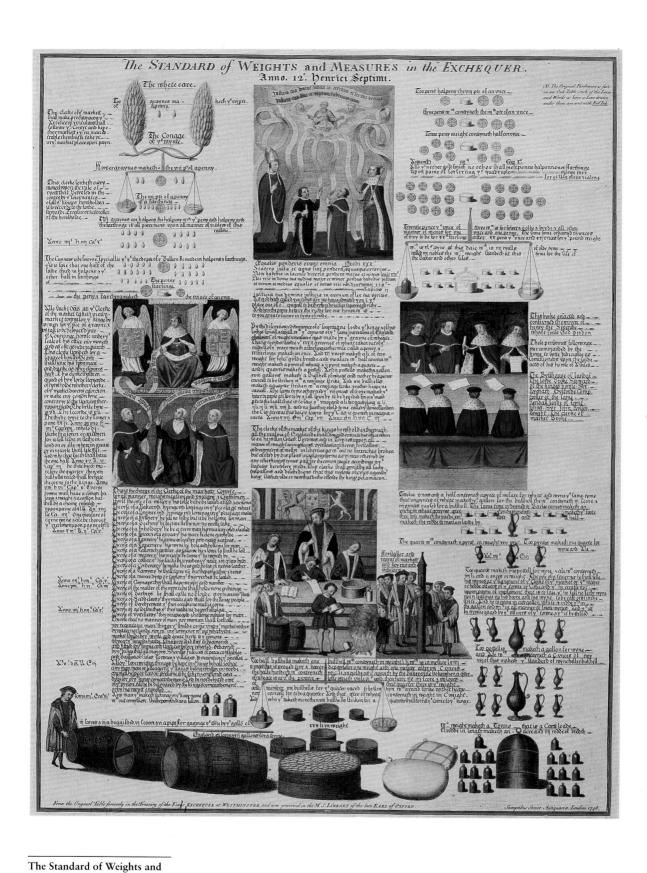

The Standard of Weights and Measures in the Exchequer of King Henry VII
Published by the Society of Antiquaries, after the original table formerly in the Treasury of the King's Exchequer at Westminster
1746
London, England
Engraving with color,
59.7 × 44.5
Collection Hugh Johnson

better than wine in partly empty ones. An ancient trick in Germany, where huge tuns were sometimes built in celebration of a particularly splendid vintage, was to drop stones in the barrel to keep the level up when wine was drawn off.

Eighteenth-century wine-drinkers were delighted to find that their wine improved, almost beyond recognition, with keeping under a cork. They soon discovered that the cork must be kept wet to remain airtight. It followed that the bottle must be kept lying down. The shape of the bottle steadily evolved, between 1700 and 1770, from the old tubby "onion," then "mallet" shape, to a cylinder, which could be easily and tidily stacked. In the interim, wine racks were made with holes for the necks of the bottles, so that the bottles could be stored upside down.

Another century was to pass before a scientific explanation was found. It was Louis Pasteur who established that oxygen was the enemy: that bacteria in wine, starved of oxygen in a sealed container, were benign. Once open to the air, they rapidly turned it to vinegar.

With or without scientific understanding, the age of connoisseurship had begun. It was largely propelled, it seems, from England. King Charles II had spent fifteen years in exile at the court of Louis XIV. On his restoration in 1660 a number of the brighter element in Paris society chose the London court as offering more scope for their inclinations. They included the Marquis de Saint-Evremond, whose particular interest lay in the wine of Champagne – long famous as some of the finest in France, but just then undergoing a marked improvement under the influence of the monk Dom Pérignon, cellarer of the Abbey of Hautvillers in the Marne Valley.

Caves at Ruinart
France
Courtesy Ruinart Père & fils, Rheims, France

The caves for storing Champagne at the Ruinart firm were formerly stone quarries created by the Romans. Once the *méthode champenoise* was perfected, these quarries were recognized as ideal for the storage of Champagne, due to their year-round coolness.

INDICE DI TVTTI LI VINI CHE SI TROVANO IN ROMA·

Maluagia	Mangiaguerra	Vino d'Oruieto
Guarnaccia	Scalea	Greco di Spoleti
Moscatello	Vino Jrancese	Vino d. Torreu
Greco di Soma	Trebiano	Vino d'Orte'
Greco di Pusilico	Aglianico	Vino di Correzze
Greco di Rasina	Vino d. Paula	Vino de Cauarini
Greco della torre'	Romania	Vino d. monte rotondo
Greco d'Ischia	Vino d. Pisotollo	Vino de la Mentana
Pusilico rosso	Porto Hercole	Vino d. formelle'
Chiazello	Vino di Rosolia	Vino di Bracciano
Centola	Razzese'	Vino di Galeri
Lagrima	Albano	Vino d. Genzano
Calabrese'	Castel Gandolfo	Vino d. Caui
Coda cauallo rosso	Marini	Vino de L'Isola
Vino San Giouanni	La Riccia	Vino d. Notona
Asprino	Frascati	Vino di Sermoneta
San Seuerino	L'anguillara	Vino d. Montefortino
Mazzacane'	Vino del monte	Vino della Molara
Vernotico	Vino de rocca de Papa	Vino d. Campagnano
Vino di Santa Rosella	Montarano	Vino Valariano
Corso di taglia moscato	Carignella	Vino d. Nezano
Corso di pietra nera	Vino d. Talaggio	Vino d. Gauignano
Corso d. Brand"	Terracina	Sauelli
Latino	Caprarola	Vino d. Sutry
Beluedere	Turpia	Vino d. Velletri
Granatino d. Spagna	Monte di S.ta Maria	Vino Petralla
Vino di Vico	Galese	Romanesco
Vino di sette terze'	Greco di Castello	Vino di monte Pulciano
Corso	Moscatello di Montefiascone	Vino arrornato
Pietra nera	Vino di Montopol	Raspato
Vino Salernitano		

It is possible to claim for Dom Pérignon the title of the first great connoisseur winemaker. His high standards and fine palate produced wines of a new subtlety and finesse. His trick was blending: the making of a *cuvée* of wines from different grapes grown in different parts of the Champagne region.

This wine was in high demand in London. It was shipped in barrels immediately after the vintage in the time-honored way, then bottled (in bottles of better quality than those being made in France) and stoppered with corks. By spring the corks were flying. Champagne, harvested in the late autumn of the cold north, rarely finishes its fermentation before winter. Spring starts the bubbles all over again – and gives the wine a "briskness," which English society found irresistible.

Tie the cork down with string, they learned, and either the bottle burst or the wine became even brisker, although rather cloudy. This, known in France today as the *méthode rurale*, was how Champagne was first made sparkling. The *méthode champenoise*, a long and laborious process to prevent cloudiness in the wine, was the product of nineteenth-century industrial ingenuity (and the invention, specifically, of the famous Veuve Clicquot).

As it turned out, the craze for sparkling Champagne was short-lived. For most of the eighteenth century the traditional still or slightly fizzy wine of the region was preferred. But the craze had other effects. It made wine and its quality a talking-point of the beau monde, and it provoked rivalry between regions and between producers – particularly for the increasingly rich English market.

So the generation that first met Champagne also met the first First

Indice di tutti li vini che si trovano in Roma
(Index of all the wines found in Rome)
c. 1630
Published by Nicholaes van Aelst
Rome, Italy
Etching, 26 × 45.7
The Seagram Museum, Waterloo, Ontario

Growth claret: the wine of Haut-Brion, which was marketed in London by a surprisingly modern device. The proprietor, Jean de Pontac, sent his son to open London's first restaurant, Pontac's Head. Samuel Pepys's curiosity took him to try the fashionable new wine. He found it had "a good and most particular taste." "Most particular"—that was the point. The notion of the individual growth, a luxury product unlike any other wine, was born.

These were the days of vast fortunes in Bordeaux. Trade with the Indies made its merchants millionaires. They soon followed Pontac's lead in planting the best gravel outcrops of the Médoc, north of the city, hitherto a "pays sauvage et solitaire," with vines. Lafite, Margaux, and Latour, the three original First Growths of the Médoc, all come into sight in the first years of the eighteenth century. Nothing, certainly not the mere fact of hostilities with France, could prevent the rapacious but undeniably stylish English aristocracy from getting its share.

Advertisements in the *London Gazette* first announced in 1703 the sale of quantities of "New French Clarets" captured by Royal Navy ships, or privateers, in the English Channel. They were sold by auction at London's coffeehouses (notably Lloyd's, which was soon to become famous as the center for marine insurance). The wines named first were Haut-Brion and Margaux. It seems unlikely that their proprietors should have entrusted their valuable wines to unarmed vessels off an enemy shore unless just such a capture and sale was what they had in mind. One of the ships captured even carried, by happy chance, a cargo of corks. (The English had bottles enough.)

What should the middle classes drink, with Claret become a rarity sold at auction? The answer, much to their disgust, was Port – a newfangled decoction of raw red wine from northern Portugal and even rawer brandy. The Methuen Treaty of 1703 gave Portugal trading privileges with Britain (which the former country still enjoys). The British did not enjoy Port – not until, bottled and cellared for ten years or more, then gingerly sampled again, it turned out to be capable of extraordinary qualities: vigor and velvet in a glass. So Port, too, was made by the happy conjunction of cork and bottle. The era of fine wines aged in the bottle had begun.

Is this repeated emphasis on England and the British market overdone? I think not. It is export that makes reputations, raises standards, and, above all, provides the driving force of profit for investment. There were other export markets: the Low Countries and northern Germany, for example. But England (and Scotland) were not only steeped in the tradition of buying the best wines to be had; with the burgeoning British Empire they could afford to call the tune.

What, meanwhile, of the rest of wine-producing Europe? In France, Burgundy was highly esteemed, but export was rare from such a land-locked vineyard. The wines of Auxerre (Chablis is the celebrated remnant) supplied Paris. Sweet Sacks, such as the Muscatel Frontignan, were exported from the Mediterranean coasts, and the strong red wine of Roussillon was appreciated.

Strong reds were much in demand for blending. It may be that the British palate was vitiated by the strength of Port, for it began to demand its Claret "stiffened" with something stronger. Hermitage from the Rhône, Roussillon, and a great deal of the darkest and most alcoholic wine from eastern Spain, Benicarlo, Priorato, or Alicante, were openly mixed with the delicate growths of the Médoc. Astonishingly, Lafite "Hermitag'd" fetched a higher price in London than Lafite pure.

Florence had long been known for the quality of its wine. Tuscan wine may even have been the first wine to be shipped in bottles, or *fiaschi,* as early as Elizabethan times. The flasks stood upright in chests, a layer of olive oil floating on the wine in place of a cork – a practice known and used in ancient Rome.

Alambic charentais
Cognac pot still
From the distillery of Bouchon-Biteaud
c. 1880
Marcel Maresté Frères
Cognac, France
Copper and brass,
230 × 480 × 160
Courtesy JAs Hennessy & Co.,
Cognac, France

Machine for filling bottles
c. 1920
Monsieur Vernhes
Cognac, France
Cast iron, copper, and brass,
91 × 82.5 × 55
Collection JAs Hennessy & Co.,
Cognac, France

This machine, which fills six
bottles at one time, was used for
bottling wine and Brandy. The
machine is fitted with a tray to
catch any spillage.

Strong Sacks were still popular, from whatever source. It was often a matter of circumstance and convenience that decided which one. Madeira, for instance, became the drink of the American colonies owing to a law of Charles II to protect English shipping. American ships were forbidden to load wine in Europe – so they loaded in Madeira, felicitously sited off the coast of Africa.

Later, Nelson found comfort for his seamen at Marsala in Sicily, and Wellington's officers, occupied in the Peninsular War, came to terms with the wines of Lisbon. Returning warriors brought their tastes home like battle honors and caused silver labels for decanters ("bottle tickets" was the contemporary term) to be wrought, often in uncouth spelling, to announce their nostalgic favorites.

It is probably Rhine wine that has had the longest and most consistent record of success. Bloody interruptions notwithstanding, the bishops and princes of the Rhineland have never seriously paused in their wine-making since Charlemagne's reign. There may indeed have been vintages somewhere along the Moselle or the Rhine every year since Roman times. Some of the world's noblest cellars, of lordly and episcopal houses, attest to it: for thirty generations and more, their vaults have sheltered a succession of the same or similar varieties of Rhine wine. The modern Riesling, introduced in the eighteenth century on the Moselle by the Von Kesselstatts of Trier, seems to be a mutation of a vine found preserved in archaeological remains of the Roman occupation. Austria, Hungary, and Romania, too, can be added to the countries that probably preserved their vines from the colonies of Roman veterans who first planted them.

It is realistic to consider the islands of Madeira and the Canaries, colonized with the vine in the fifteenth century, as the final expansion of the

Mediterranean vineyard. The vine, you might say, had regained Atlantis. Now it was the turn of the New World and recently established colonies.

It is a fascinating speculation to ask oneself: What would have happened if any of the French explorers in the New World had established vineyards? As the masters of wine, indeed the creators of the concept of wine of special and luxurious quality, I cannot imagine that they would have been content with such primitive brews as were the founders of the new colonies of the vine.

But the shifts of history gave the privilege of transplanting the vine, from its headquarters in Europe to its overseas outposts, to peoples lacking either experience or discrimination in viticulture: to first the Spanish, then the Dutch, then the English.

The first planting of the vine in the New World can be dated with confidence very early in the sixteenth century in Mexico, the "New Spain" governed by the conqueror Cortez. Rather than rely on expensive shipments from Spain or the Canary Islands, Cortez in 1524 decreed that every Spaniard with a land grant must plant vines and make wine, both for the religious sacrament and as an essential part of the diet.

It was clearly a success. By the middle of the sixteenth century the new Spanish territories of Peru, Chile, and Argentina were all making their own wine – too much for the liking of the government in Spain. Like Domitian fifteen hundred years before, King Philip II acted, without effect, to protect the Spanish wine trade by forbidding new vineyards in America. In 1593 the first commercial *bodega* (wine supplier) in America, to our present knowledge, was started at Parras in Coahuila state, north of Mexico City. Today its buildings are once again in use for wine-making and the production of brandy.

In Argentina the Criollas, in Chile the País, in Mexico the Mission grape, apparently the original coarse grape used by the early settlers, is still grown – and in great quantities. Its wine is terrible. Do not be tempted to try it.

Why this particular variety was transported to the colonies, when Spain has so many varieties of better quality, we shall probably never know. What is certain is that it condemned these Spanish colonial vineyards to third-class status for the first three hundred years of their exis-

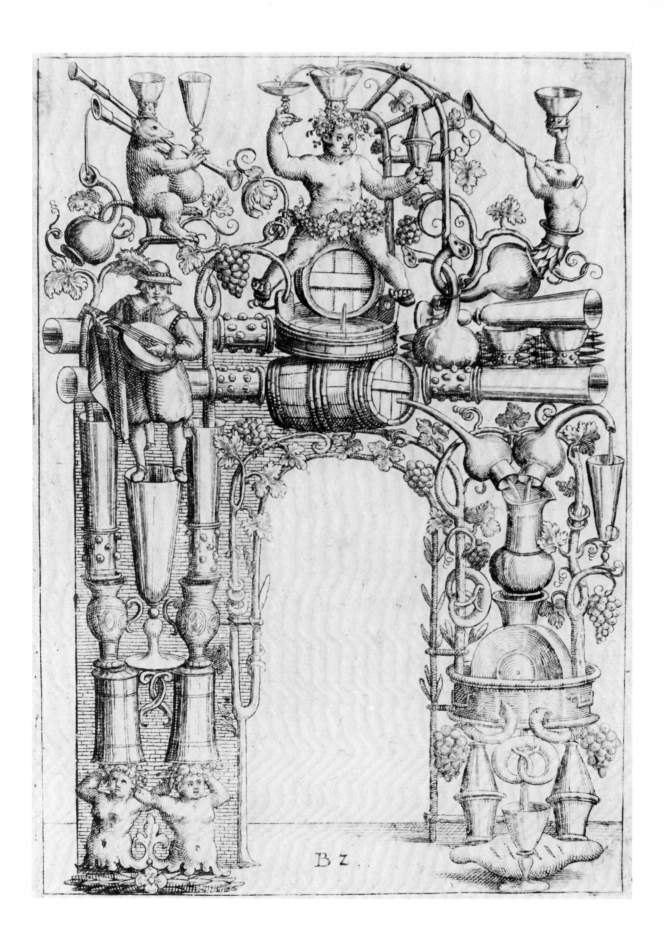

B z.

tence. One possible explanation is simply the jealousy of the mother country – for independence from Spain was rapidly followed (at least in Argentina and Chile) by the importation of better vines.

Unexpectedly, it was the Dutch who first made fine wine in their new colonies – and not in any extensive settlement but at their little trading and victualing outpost at the Cape of Good Hope, the newly founded Cape Colony, in the last years of the seventeenth century. The first governor, Simon van der Stel, gave the name of Constantia to his beautiful state on the southern slopes of Table Mountain. His successors, over the next one hundred years, capitalized on the extravagant farming methods he used (slave labor was cheap) to create a superior wine, in fact the first *Grand Cru* of the new colonies.

Constantia was a very sweet dessert wine made either of red or white Muscat grapes. Its quality was universally acknowledged, not only by the many visitors to the Cape (every ship going to India or beyond stopped for provisions, and every passenger of rank seems to have visited Constantia) but by the merchants of northern Europe and their best customers, including Frederick the Great and Napoleon. If I may hazard a guess at the reason for its outstanding quality, for which there is more than enough evidence, it lay not only in appropriate soil and situation but in very heavy investment by the owners. The vineyard was enriched every year with manure dug in in trenches. Continuous shifts of workers removed insect pests in the vineyard by hand. The grapes and the wine-making apparatus were kept impeccably clean.

We can draw some conclusions from all this about the reason for the unique place of Constantia among early wines of the new colonies. The vineyard was run like a First Growth. But this was only possible because of the existence of a rich, demanding, and critical market (in passing ships, and, back in Holland, among the directors of the Dutch East India Company). No great wine is ever made without rich patronage.

Why did it stop? It was, I am sorry to say, due to the greed of the officials, first of the Dutch East India Company, and then of the British government. When the Cape was ceded to Britain all the high government officers regarded a free supply of the best Cape wine as a perquisite of office. Nobody can run a vineyard on this basis. (Happily, I can provide a tasting footnote: my one experience of Constantia was a pint bottle of the 1805 vintage, drunk in 1967. The wine was still lusciously rich, of distinctly smoky, only faintly Muscat, character, and prodigiously fine.)

At the beginning of the nineteenth century, then, vineyards were widely spread in the new colonies, but fine wine was virtually unknown.

Residence, Vineyards and Orchards of Geo. F. Hooper, Sonoma, California
From *Illustrated Atlas of California*, 1876
Lithograph, 19.2 × 40.6
The Seagram Museum, Waterloo, Ontario

Spring Mountain Winery
Napa Valley, California
Courtesy Edmund Osterland and the Wine Institute

The new Australians were the most wine-minded of colonists. The ship carrying the first governor (and the first batch of convicts) to Botany Bay in 1788 also carried vine plants. Fifteen years later, the first issue of Australia's first newspaper, the *Sydney Gazette*, published a page of directions on how to plant a vineyard. By 1822 viticulture had reached the point that wines from New South Wales were exhibited at the Royal Society of Arts in London and awarded a silver medal. The future looked promising. What was needed was research to suit old vine varieties to the new conditions.

The first important methodical work on this vital theme was undertaken by a young Australian, James Busby, who from 1831 to 1833 toured first Spain and then France, learning all he could about viticulture and wine-making. To his surprise, his French hosts showed nothing but eagerness to help him. At the Botanic Garden at Montpellier alone he was given some 400 varieties of vine, and 133 more at the Royal Luxembourg Nurseries in Paris. Busby catalogued his vines precisely and distributed them generously. To him belongs the title of the father of Australian wine. Within thirty years of his visit to Europe, a large proportion of the eventual fine-wine areas of Australia were planted, and many of the families whose names are today household words in Australia – Hardy, Gramp, Penfold, Seppelt, Hill-Smith, Tyrell – were established wine-makers.

By chance, it was at precisely the same time as Busby's voyage that the

**Moët & Chandon Champagne
White Star**
1899
Alphonse Mucha (1860–1933)
France
Lithograph, 61 × 23
Collection Moët & Chandon,
Epernay, France

Moët & Chandon
Orangerie

Moët & Chandon
Hôtels Particuliers

**Moët et Chandon Croisant La
Veuve Clicquot
(Moët and Chandon Encounter
the Widow Clicquot)**
From *Le Figaro*, May 1, 1966
Chaval
France
Courtesy Agence IDEREA,
Paris, © 1976

Moët et Chandon croisant la veuve Clicquot

first efforts were made to grow grapes of quality in California. Here the pioneer was a Frenchman, happily named Jean-Louis Vignes, who imported French vines and struggled in the hot climate of Los Angeles to make drinkable wine and brandy.

The far more suitable vine-growing climate of northern California was not discovered until the Gold Rush of 1848 gave rise to the new city of San Francisco. The Sonoma and Napa valleys to the north of San Francisco Bay proved far superior to the Los Angeles basin as vineyards. The James Busby of California was the Hungarian count and colonel Agoston Haraszthy, who made expeditions to Europe in 1851 and 1861, returning from the second with 100,000 vine cuttings of 300 varieties. Haraszthy's Sonoma property, Buena Vista, became the pioneer of quality wine in California. It still exists, at least in name, today. Within the next thirty years (that is, one generation later than in Australia), many of the best-known houses in California wine, including Almaden, Beringer, Paul Masson, Concannon, Inglenook, Schramsberg, Charles Krug, Mirassou, Simi, and Wente Brothers, came into existence.

There is no doubt as to the high quality of the wine the Californians made in the later years of the last century. Many won prizes in European competitions. It was rapidly discovered that the Cabernet Sauvignon was the supremely suitable grape for the Napa Valley. Deep cellars were cut in the hillsides by Chinese coolies to provide the essential cool conditions for maturing. All this investment in quality was made possible by the existence of a rich and demanding local market, the booming city of San Francisco.

It is a sad fact that Australia's wine-makers were for nearly a century discouraged from making the necessary effort by the indifference and

CROQUIS VARIÉS

— A la santé du raisin ! . . puisse-t-il ne pas être malade cette année!

stinginess of their principal customers, the British. It is even more tragic that America, by introducing the folly of Prohibition, should have murdered its own flourishing and excellent wine industry.

It is often said that wine-making progressed hardly at all between the Middle Ages and the start of the twentieth century, and that certain practices still found today, indeed, in backward areas, are as old as European civilization. This may be when it comes to the farming side of the business; a cow is a cow, for Pliny or for us, and so is a vine a vine, to be planted, pruned, and cultivated.

As we have seen, though, the seventeenth century began to understand that wine was capable of apparently limitless improvement. Money spent on bettering vineyards and cellars paid off handsomely in an expanding market. The eighteenth century saw the development of natural wines — wine with no additives — with all their subtlety and beauty of flavor. When the Industrial Revolution arrived, it brought a new phenomenon: organized large-scale production for a new middle-class market.

Once again it was Champagne that led the way. Rationalized techniques, vast cellars, brand names, advertising, and an international sales force made the fortunes of the widow Clicquot, the Moëts, and a score of other Champagne houses. From about 1820 onward the industrialized "winery" came into being, and was repeated, with variations, all over the world.

Very splendid and extravagant are its monuments. Its styles range from the faux-châteaux of Champagne to the titanic aisles of the sherry *bodegas,* from the labyrinthine "lodges" of the port shippers to the vast stone barns of the Napa Valley, from the gray dignity of Bordeaux's Quai des Chartrons to flirtations with Art Nouveau in Rioja and Catalonia.

The wine industry flowered prodigiously in the nineteenth century. And, with the inevitability of Greek tragedy, it was brought low. Two great scourges swept through the vineyards: downy mildew and phylloxera — the latter a mere mite, but a mite that, over the closing thirty years of the last century, destroyed and caused the replanting of almost every vineyard in the world. In desperation many were planted in the wrong places, with the wrong vines.

Daumier's cartoons chronicle the times. Two Frenchmen are tasting. Says one, "This wine smells like water." Says the other, "You're wrong, it's water that smells like wine."

World war, Prohibition, recession, even a long run of poor vintages followed phylloxera. Hard as it is to believe, for over half a century, with

Getrait Aecker, Wein Gärten und Bienen-Zucht (Agriculture, Vineyards and Bee-Keeping)
Plate 5 from the series *Allerhand Neu erfundene Comperts*
1743
Johann Justin Preisler
(1698–1771)
Nuremberg, Germany
Etching, 19.7 × 15.8
Cooper-Hewitt Museum, New York. Gift of Eleanor and Sarah Hewitt, 1925-2-473

a few notable exceptions, the heart (and the profitability) went out of the wine business. Right up to the end of the 1950s even the world's best wines were going begging. The patient *vigneron* struggled on, unappreciated. He little knew then where help would come from, or suspected that in the universities of California and Australia studies were going on that would revolutionize the wine industry the world over.

This is not the place to chronicle the technological revolution of wine. It centered at first on fitting vine varieties to climates, then on controlling the temperature of fermentation. In viticulture it embraces the cloning and virus-treating of vines, new trellising and pruning systems, new frost-protection measures, new sprays and treatments, new mechanical picking methods, and more.

In oenology, temperature may be the most important single factor, but pressing techniques, the study of yeasts, ways of clarifying juice, understanding how wine ages and the effect of barrels have all contributed to the revolution.

Specifically, they have made good wine possible – and bad wine unnecessary – in almost every region where the vine is planted.

It remained for the market to reawaken, demand quality, and pay for it. When the moment came, in the 1960s, we all know how spectacular the renaissance was. Within a decade regions and even countries with no or few fine-wine traditions were measuring themselves against the classic wines of Europe. The classics in their turn were demanded everywhere, and once again turned the profit they generated into higher quality. We stand, it seems, at the gates of a golden age. The technology is ready, the capacity in place. Only one thing can fail us now – and that is the demand. When wine is properly seen as the blessing it can be, that too will be secure. It is a sin to spurn the gift of the gods.

44

Visions of the Vine:
A Symbolic History

Dora Jane Janson

Hebe Pouring Wine for Jupiter
c. 1810–23
Felice Giani (1760–1823)
Italy
Pen and brown ink, brown
wash, and graphite, 25.6 × 25.4
Cooper-Hewitt Museum, New
York. Friends of the Museum
Fund, 1901-39-3467

The Last Supper
1509–11
Albrecht Dürer (1471–1528)
Germany
Woodcut, 14.3 × 10.9
Cooper-Hewitt Museum, New
York. Gift of Leo Wallerstein,
1951-170-8

The grape, over the course of history, has carried two paramount associations. It is a fruit of promise: when Moses sent his spies to reconnoiter the Promised Land, they brought back a cluster of grapes so large that it had to be carried on a pole between two men. Even more indelible is the grape's sybaritic association: women feeding them one by one to dissipated nobles at Roman orgies. Indeed, so strong is this image that in the film *I'm No Angel*, when Mae West, considering the plea of her latest suitor, tells her maid, "Beulah, peel me a grape," we know exactly what she has in mind. Implicit in both of these associations are the qualities of abundance, wealth, and sensuality.

The grape appears as the gift of the earth, affording instant enjoyment. Wine is a much more complex proposition; a great deal of time and labor intervene before grapes turn into wine. The fruit must be harvested at the peak of perfection and hauled to the press, where its juice is extracted; when the liquid ferments, it is then poured carefully into containers, whether the terra-cotta amphorae of the Mediterranean coastal peoples or the wooden casks and barrels of the more northerly Europeans.

At some point, this agreeable bland beverage becomes a potion with a myriad of different aromas – on the tongue, in the nostrils, and finally in a sort of combined sensory memory. The process leads to speculation about the mysterious life that inhabits simple grape juice, causing such a wondrous transformation. No less awesome is its effect on the body and mind of the drinker. Whatever we do not comprehend, good or bad, combines the attraction and the fear of the unknown. A little wizardry is imputed to those who know how to supply wine, and our species has never stopped either drinking or thinking about it. *Vit*, the Latin root that we recognize in the word "viticulture" – a word that appears frequently in these pages – is also the source of *vita*, or life itself. Wine inspirits and inspires, breathing life into our existence. From the little we know about our own history on earth, wine has been a part of it, as both reward and sacrifice, from early days.

The eminent science historian D. J. de Solla Prince argued that great breakthroughs in science are not produced by deliberate ratiocination and logic but by sheer chance or as the by-product of a different goal. The appearance of wine thousands of years ago may have been just such a fortuitous accident, dependent upon the fermentation of naturally occurring yeasts on the skins of grapes. Viticulture in all of its aspects has radically changed the history of society, its miracle wrought long before the scientific basis of wine-making was recognized or fully understood. And, as can be seen from even the most cursory glance at the history of art, the impact of wine on culture has been more dramatic than its effect on science.

The Drunkenness of Noah
From Hartmann Schedel, *Liber Cronicarum (The Nuremberg Chronicle)*, Nuremberg, 1493
Michael Wohlgemuth (1434–1519) or Wilhelm Pleydenwurff
Germany
Woodcut, 44.5 × 30
Cooper-Hewitt Museum Library, New York

Wine was rapidly embraced as a magical fluid. As such, it nourished the imagination and inspired the growth of myths and legends. Wine also came to play a major role in many religions; both wine and its source – the grapevine – assumed their place as central symbols of power, continuity, and even resurrection. Wine may be considered by most of us to be a pleasant companion of daily life; in past millenniums, however, wine and vine were symbols that cut across many boundaries of geography and time. The gods of the ancient world, whose personalities we can only vaguely apprehend through images that survive today, were often linked by wine to important rituals and beliefs. The religious systems of both Judaism and Christianity also include wine as a primary symbol. In the history of art can be found many common threads of meaning that link symbols and cultures over the centuries. Among them are images, narratives, motifs, and patterns that celebrate the vine and its rich abundance.

In vino veritas goes the old Latin saying, but you cannot scoop these verities with a ladle; rather, it is the truth that resides within us, individually and collectively, that wine has helped to release. Wine may give form to our dreams, offering a way to merge the world of flesh with that of the spirit. Its undeniable power to intoxicate has also revealed many of our deep-seated fears and concerns. As we look at the history of wine and vine as depicted in the arts of over five thousand years, the complex nature and significance of this special fluid may be suggested, along with the contours and textures of our shared human culture.

Most of us are familiar with the biblical narrative of the Flood, whose sole survivors were Noah and his family (along with a menagerie of paired animals). After landing safely on Mount Ararat, Noah "planted a vineyard; and he drank of the wine and became drunk." Not only does this account lead one to conclude that viticulture and wine-making must have been skills already integrated into the daily lives of people prior to the Flood – and these skills were transmitted to future generations through the agricultural and viticultural expertise of Noah – it also points out that viticulture was among the first of the agricultural activities to be resumed. The fact that Noah planted a vineyard makes the grape a poignant symbol of continuity and, in a certain sense, of resurrection and rebirth after destruction. The regenerative power of the vine, which emerges fresh and vital each spring from an apparently dead rootstock, serves to embody the hope of continuity.

The story of Noah also reveals another aspect of wine's history – the effect of the drink on the drinker. Without laboring the point, it should be noted that the drunkenness of Noah also serves to emphasize the power of the drink to affect reason and behavior. It was this aspect of Noah's viticultural recreation, rather than his landmark efforts at grape-growing, that seems to have found a particular appeal in the popular imagery of later centuries.

As the story of Noah follows immediately after the Creation of the world in the biblical account, it must be one of the most ancient of legends. An older version of the story of the Great Flood is to be found in the *Epic of Gilgamesh*, generally agreed to date around 3000 B.C. Gilgamesh was a ruler of Mesopotamia, the land lying between the Euphrates and Tigris rivers, and known to be one of the early homes of viticulture. Just downstream from Nineveh, one of the greatest of Mesopotamian cities – not far from Ararat – was the royal cemetery of Ur. In this important site has been found evidence of a material and artistic culture that documents the well-being of the elite. Included in the archaeological finds at Ur was the soundbox of a harp (dated c. 2600 B.C.) inlaid with scenes of merrymaking and feasting. Of particular interest is a section of this pictorial narrative that shows a lion about to drink from a spouted cup borne aloft in his right paw. Although it is not clear that the cup contains wine, the ritual and ceremonial choreography of drinking is apparent. If this is indeed a "royal" beast whose status reflects the hierarchy and mythology of the culture, then the "royal" drink is an equally important symbol. As will be seen in the art history of wine, the symbolic purpose of ritual drinking continues over the millenniums and is familiar to us in the ceremonies of kiddush and the sacrament of the Eucharist.

The Ship of Bacchus and Orpheus
From a series of designs for mock naval battles for the wedding festivities of Cosimo II de Medici
1608
Remigio Cantagallina (c. 1582–c. 1635), after Giulio Parigi (d. 1635)
Florence, Italy
Etching, 18.3 × 28.7
Cooper-Hewitt Museum, New York. Gift of Mrs. William Greenough, 1941-49-31

This etching combines the story of Dionysus' kidnapping by sailors and his subsequent triumph over his captors by turning the ship into a living vineyard with the related story of Orpheus, who returned successfully from the underworld.

O RFEO CONDOTTO DA BACCO
Barca del Sig. Nicolo Berardi
Remigio Canta Gallina F.
Battaglia Navale rapp. in Arno per le nozze del Ser.mo Principe di Toscana l'anno 1608 Giulio Parigi I.

Bowl
6th–7th century
Iran, Sasanian
Silver with niello, 16.3 × 9.8
Norbert Schimmel Collection,
New York

The association of a running ti-
gress with grapevines suggests a
Dionysiac context for this bowl.

Toutes les Saisons
1707
Jacobus Coelemans (c. 1654–
c. 1735), after Jean Miel (1599–
1664)
France
Engraving, 29.5 × 35
Courtesy Lungarotti Winery Pri-
vate Collection, Museo del Vino,
Torgiano, Italy

The four figures depicted are
Ceres, goddess of agriculture,
who holds a sheaf of wheat,
Venus, Cupid, and a skin-draped
Bacchus.

Kylix
Shallow two-handled cup
Attributed to the Painter of
Brussels R 330
460–450 B.C.
Greece
Pottery, red-figured decoration,
12 × 27
The Metropolitan Museum of
Art, New York. Rogers Fund,
1919

The *kylix* is decorated in the
center with a youth being served
wine in a shallow cup. The scene
probably takes place at a sym-
posium, a drinking party following the evening meal, where
music, games, and conversation
prevailed.

Among the gods and goddesses of the ancient world, few have made as
strong an impression as Dionysus, the Greek god of wine. The story of
Dionysus, which certainly ranks among the most significant in the history of wine, begins with his extraordinary birth. Zeus, after fathering
the child with a mortal woman, who was destroyed by asking her immortal lover to reveal himself in his glory, saved the unborn child by
sewing him into his thigh; thus Dionysus was known as the "twice-
born," a miracle of a special sort. Raised by nymphs, the young Dionysus
traveled to Phrygia (Asia Minor) where he was instructed in the rites of
worship of Rhea, the mother goddess. Discovering the vine and the way
to extract the juice from the fruits to create wine, Dionysus traversed
Asia, as far as India it was said, stopping along the way to teach people
how to grow grapes and make wine and, at the same time, according to
Homer, "establishing my mysteries and rites that I might be revealed on
earth for what I am: a god."

Returning to Greece after several years, he expected to claim his right-
ful place as the son of Zeus; instead, he encountered doubt and rejection.
Fleeing to the island of Dia, he was discovered by some sailors. Thinking
the handsome youth to be a noble, the sailors took him captive. They
planned to hold him for ransom or, if that failed, to sell him as a slave in
Egypt. When asked where he would like to be taken, Dionysus said that
he wanted to go to Naxos. The sailors stealthily set a different course, to
Egypt. Suddenly their boat stopped in mid-ocean. In vain the sailors
spread more sail and pulled harder at the oars; the boat could not be
moved. They found that ivy had twined itself around the oars, and that
the mast was encased in a grapevine full of heavy clusters of grapes. The
air was heavy with the smell of wine. The captive god stood up, his head
wreathed in vine leaves, while tigers and panthers played at his feet. The
terrified crew jumped overboard and were transformed into dolphins.
The powerful god had suddenly revealed himself, bringing a halt to the
activities of men, and changing the world of reason and logic into one of
mystery and terror.

The story of Dionysus' kidnapping and miraculous triumph over his
captors must antedate any of the pictorial sources that record the narrative, but it is not likely to have originated much before 1250 B.C., when
we know that the Greek kingdom Mycenae had a lively commerce with
Egypt, which probably included slaves. Compared to Ur and Nineveh,
this is a fairly recent date; however, the allusion to his visit with Rhea,

Bacchanal
1640
Giovanni Andrea Podesta
(c. 1620–c. 1673)
Italy
Etching, 26.4 × 39.2
Courtesy Lungarotti Winery Private Collection, Museo del Vino, Torgiano, Italy

A veritable free-for-all occurs in this lively image of a Bacchanal. While satyrs and putti tread grapes and followers bear a vine-draped wreath, the tipsy Bacchus/Silenus figure is carried toward a wine vat.

the timeless mother goddess, hints at a far earlier source for the cult of Dionysus. The so-called Cup of the Ptolemies, carved of banded agate and dated to the first century B.C., shows the appurtenances of Rhea's cult on one side and the symbols and props of the Dionysiac mysteries on the other. Around the altar of Dionysus are depicted an assortment of wine vessels, one of which has overturned, spilling the liquid. The liquid is probably wine, and it is being lapped by a panther, the animal identified with Dionysus. The spilled liquid suggests a libation, and possibly a substitute for blood sacrifice.

The animals with which Dionysus was most closely associated were members of the feline family – panthers, tigers, and leopards – the sleek and stealthy hunters of flesh. It is not unusual to see representations of his followers wearing panther or leopard skins. The origins of both the Dionysiac cult and that of the mother goddess seem to lead us to what is now Turkey. In Çatal Hüyük, a site that dates back to 6000 B.C., one of the oldest mural paintings (excepting those in caves) has been discovered. The image shows a running male figure holding a rodlike instrument or weapon. Whether warrior or dancer, the young man is clad in the skin of a spotted leopard, tied at neck and waist, and billowing out behind him as he runs. This may be the ancestor of many later depictions of the devotees of the wine god, who likewise radiate the athletic energy of their ritual celebrations.

Dionysus combined in his persona two rather different aspects of the grape and wine: on the one hand, he was a god of physical pleasure and ecstasy, clearly related to the fertility of the vine and the celebration of earthly pleasures available through intoxication; the other aspect, darker and more sinister, revolved around the destructive and terror-inspiring actions of his devotees.

The Age of Fable, Bulfinch's classic, has served a number of generations as a basic narrative of the exploits of the gods, and it includes mention of the "wild, uproarious following" that celebrated the god in annual rites "with thyrsus-rods and torches in their hands, singing and shouting amid the clash and jar of cymbals and flutes." One can draw a parallel between such behavior and the frenzied and passionate actions of followers of pop singers (today called "groupies"; in my own day, we were called "bobby-soxers," whose idol was Frank Sinatra!). Physiologists have now recognized that a euphoric state may be related to the release of a substance called endorphin into the bloodstream; certainly the same intensity of pleasure and excitation in the ancient Bacchanals had a basis in physiology, but wine assisted in achieving this state.

Nijinsky in "L'Après-Midi d'un Faune"
1912
Original photograph by Baron Adolphe de Meyer (1868–1949)
Palladium print by Richard Benson (b. 1943)
20.5 × 15.5
Courtesy Washburn Gallery, New York

Bacchus
1771
Gabriel Müller, after Hendrick Goltzius (1558–1617)
Austria
Engraving, 24.8 × 18.5
The Seagram Museum, Waterloo, Ontario

Although the Dionysiac revels may have some parallels in the patterns of culture today, they must have done something worse than disturb the peace and quiet of the neighborhood, for the celebrations of Dionysus were severely limited to specific times. The followers of the god of wine often inspired fear and hatred among the populace by their wanton destructiveness of life – both animal and human – and by their propensity for eating raw flesh.

It is important to remember that Dionysus was also the god of theater, and one may ask what the connection may be with wine. Drama, especially tragedies, can break down the everyday repression of our emotions, thus relieving us by releasing them. In Greek, this was called "catharsis." The properties of wine, as we have seen, can achieve a similar effect on individuals, but in the theater the experience is "ritualized"; through drama, the uncontrollable aspects of human behavior are, in one sense, neutralized by becoming a substitute for action. We are a part of the drama, and yet we are separate. This idea appears in concrete form in the masks that emblemize theater. If we followed them back to their origins, we might find that they were once real heads, preserved for ancestor worship or the display of vanquished enemies. Once again, a primitive ritual is displaced by an activity that links a society together. The figure of Dionysus, with his duality of intent and meaning, is the logical matrix for such an experience.

At his most harmless, Dionysus was nothing more than the giver of wine (in which form he was primarily celebrated by the Romans in the guise of Bacchus, a tamed-down version of this awe-inspiring and powerful force). He was, of course, closely identified with the world of plants through the vine itself, and the perpetual cycle of growth, harvest, and decline on an annual basis that the grapevine so clearly expressed. Dionysus was both man and god; his nature also encompassed both humans and animals; ecstasy and brutality were brought together in one personality, as were pleasure and madness. Dionysus was identified with the paradox of human behavior – on one side creative and productive, and on the other destructive and uncontrollable. It was wine that made

Kantharos
Deep two-handled cup
Showing Dionysus seated in a
grape arbor
c. 340–320 B.C.
Apulia, Italy
Pottery, red-figured decoration,
13.5 × 10.5
Museum of Fine Arts, Boston.
Gift of Thomas G. Appleton

Roman column fragment
1st century
Speyer, Germany
Stone, diameter 1 meter
Courtesy Historisches Museum
der Pfalz, Speyer

Reputed to be from a monument
for Jupiter, this column depicts
the harvester of grapes wielding
a *serpette*, with which the clusters are severed from the vine.
The entwined branches of the
vine encircle a spread-tailed peacock. Although these symbols
are here used in a Roman context, both vine and peacock
were used in Christian art to
symbolize immortality; the vine
was resurrected each spring, and
the flesh of the peacock was believed to be immune from decay.

**Relief fragment from a
sarcophagus**
4th century
Early Christian
Marble, 38.5 × 57.3
Courtesy The Metropolitan Mu-
seum of Art, New York. Fletcher
Fund, 1924

The putti laboring in the vines
was a motif inherited from Roman art; here the funeral context suggests the use of the motif
as a symbol of resurrection and
eternal life.

Dionysus a living reality inside the minds of his followers; whereas most other gods were distant and separate, Dionysus alone "lived" in his followers.

This aspect of the Dionysiac mysteries may have planted the idea of immortality, as the annual resurrection of the vine no doubt inspired ideas of resurrection and rebirth. The ancients, whether Babylonian, Greek, Israelite, or Roman, did not elaborate on ideas about life after death. Only the Egyptians had a "Book of the Dead," which was a sort of guidebook to the afterlife. They hoped to live as well (if not better) in the Beyond as they had on earth: hence the elaborate measures taken to preserve the corpse through mummification and to supply the deceased with all of the necessities, utensils, and furnishings they would require in their next life. They also had a soul image – a bird with a human head – and, in addition, the idea of a ghost, as shadow, who would continue to inhabit the tomb. In a sense their god Osiris, who died yearly when the Nile's waters dried up, only to come alive again in order to feed his people when the freshets flowed, is a prototype of Christ. Theban tombs are painted with scenes of viticulture and wine-making, and many wine jars have been found in Egyptian tombs; these attest to the importance of wine in the Nile Delta. At least one could be assured that the elect of this world would probably be the elect of the next world, and wine was one of the symbols of this status and position.

This role of wine brings to mind other symbolic purposes ascribed to the drink, purposes that are clearly identified with the perpetuation of life after death. If the thought of immortality, for better or for worse, was foreign in places where wine was plentiful, but a salient part of religion where it was scarce, how did the two ideas merge? The alternative to life beyond death is eternal youth, if only the secret could be found! The gods whom the Romans took over from Greek belief were immortal, of

course, and they could confer immortality on humans (usually by installing them in the heavens as a star or constellation).

In contrast, the Dionysiac notion of resurrection and rebirth is cyclical. The continuity of the vine from season to season and from generation to generation offered a parallel to the cyclical nature of life itself. Although the vine was pruned severely each autumn (one might even say dismembered), it miraculously returned from the dead to produce its harvest. In this sense, Dionysus himself served as a supernatural example of this mystery.

Since the vine could symbolize the resurrection and continuity of life, it is not surprising to see it used frequently in funeral contexts. Many grave markers and memorials, particularly those of the Roman period, include grapevines in their designs or show actual events from the vintage, such as the gathering or treading of grapes. The perpetuation of the vine blended with the hope of perpetuation of the spirit, and certainly with the continuity of memory. Likewise, the motif was rapidly absorbed into the iconography of the early Christian Church, where the vine not only relates to the concepts of resurrection and perpetuation embraced by the ancient world but also to the new theology of the Christian Church: "I am the vine, ye are the branches: He that abideth in me, and I in him, the same bringeth forth much fruit. . . ." (John 15:5).

Although somewhat diluted by so many competing sects, the original Dionysiac mysteries still held more promise of eternal life than most other cults. One of the clearest ideas of eternal life is expressed in the cult of Orpheus, who managed to gain access to the underworld and return from it alive. The cult of Orpheus was an offshoot of the worship of Dionysus/Zagreus – a sort of mirror-image or anti-Dionysus, for his cult was in all ways the opposite of Dionysus/Bacchus, which, as we have seen, welled up out of violence, and was at best hedonistic. (It is proba-

Plaque
c. 1st century B.C.
Palmyra, Syria, Parthian
Terra-cotta, 2.8 × 3.8
The Metropolitan Museum of
Art, New York. Gift of Mr. and
Mrs. Harry G. Friedman, 1955

The draped figure on this small
plaque reclines beneath a verdant grapevine lush with fruit. A
similar depiction is known in an
Early Christian catacomb in
which Jonah is shown resting
under a vine after his miraculous
escape from the belly of a great
fish.

bly no coincidence that Orpheus, although he successfully braved the
underworld, met his end at the hands of wild Bacchantes, who tore him
limb from limb.) Dionysus/Zagreus, on the other hand, believed in a
divine soul. However, one could achieve eternal bliss only by initiation
into his cult, which, in striking contrast to the wild ways of the Bacchantes, stressed asceticism (to the point of eating no meat at all), the
virtuous life under moral and ethical rule, and the purification of the soul
through transmigration. Here the substitution of wine for blood takes on
special meaning, and the stage is set for the Last Supper of Jesus and his
apostles. For the Christian sacrament of Communion is clearly linked to
the ancient power of the vine, but it has undergone a transformation that
joins the believer to God in a new and intimate way:

> *And as they were eating, Jesus took bread, and blessed it, and brake it,
> and gave it to the disciples, and said, "Take, eat; this is my body." And
> he took the cup, and gave thanks, and gave it to them, saying, "Drink
> ye all of it; For this is my blood of the new testament, which is shed
> for many for the remission of sins" (Matthew 26: 26–28).*

Wine in the Christian sacrament, as well as in the Jewish tradition,
also symbolizes the fulfillment of a promise. The roots of this meaning
can be traced throughout both the Old and New Testaments. Some of
these representations can be found in the subterranean catacombs (meaning "tombs down under") that were used by early Christians as chapels
for their secret meetings and services. One of these ceilings depicts the
well-known story of Jonah, whose emergence from the belly of a great
fish was viewed – much as Orpheus' return from Hades – as a sort of
miracle that foretold Christ's resurrection. Here Jonah is depicted resting
under a grape arbor following his deliverance, a motif that also appears
in the art of Syria. As far as I can tell there is no equivalent illustration of
the peace that prevailed during King Solomon's reign, expressed in
I Kings 4:25 as "Each man under his own vine and fig tree"; but in each
case that we have discussed, the vine stands not only for safety after an
unusual, if not miraculous, escape from terror, but also the eternal fulfillment of God's promise. Such, too, is the promise of the wine that is the
blood of Christ.

As mentioned earlier, a pertinent example of the grape as a fulfilled
promise is to be found in the Book of Numbers 13: 23. When the Isra-
elites were within sight of the Promised Land, Moses ordered scouts to

The Antioch Chalice
First half 6th century
Syria?, Early Christian
Silver-gilt, height 19
Courtesy The Metropolitan Museum of Art, New York. The Cloisters Collection, 1950

Plate
16th century
Germany
Brass, diameter 39.5
The Metropolitan Museum of Art, New York. Rogers Fund, 1921

Caleb and Joshua, two spies sent out by Moses to survey the Promised Land, returned with a cluster of grapes of unusual size. This image, particularly popular during the medieval and later periods, was used on domestic objects ranging from metal plates to earthenware tiles.

Bonad
Wall hanging
Showing the Marriage at Cana
Early 19th century
Sweden
Painted linen tabby, 115 × 83.8
Cooper-Hewitt Museum, New
York. Gift of Richard Cranch
Greenleaf, 1959-140-6

Bonader were displayed at weddings and on other festive occasions in Sweden. At Cana, Christ
miraculously transformed water
into wine.

Ecclesiastical Cape
Used on a figure of the Infant
Christ
Early 19th century
Southern Europe
Silk moiré, embroidered with
chenille, sequins, and metal
thread, 30.5 × 56
Cooper-Hewitt Museum, New
York. Gift of Maria Cannon,
1899-2-6

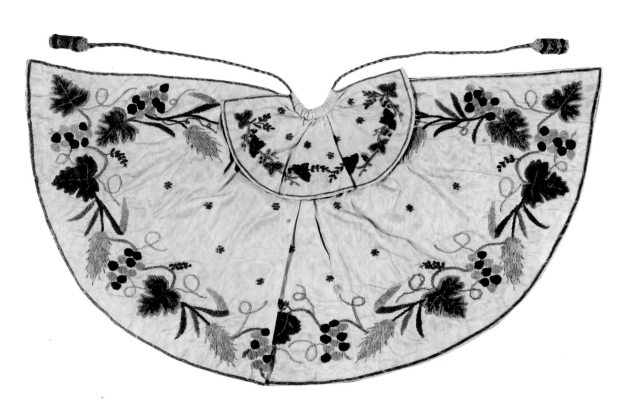

Tapestry-woven textile
Showing a Tree of Life
4th–5th century
Coptic
Wool and linen, 21.5 × 16.5
The Brooklyn Museum, New
York. Gift of Pratt Institute

The vine issuing from the urn
bears rich clusters of grapes, and
one cluster is being nibbled by a
hare. Both the grape and the
hare are associated with the concept of continuity and fertility.

Orphrey panel
Embroidered with the Tree of
Jesse
Third quarter of the 14th cen-
tury
England
Linen and colored silks, 99 × 77
Courtesy The Cleveland Mu-
seum of Art. Purchase from the
J. H. Wade Fund

survey the territory. Upon their return, two of the men – Caleb and Joshua – carried a cluster of grapes so heavy and so immense that it had to be slung over a pole and carried between them. The vital symbol of the grape, with its promise of fertility, nourishment, and continuity, became a living proof that God had kept the covenant that he had made with Moses and with his people. Another covenant, that of marriage, is symbolized by wine in the New Testament story of the Marriage at Cana.

The grapevine is also a prominent part of the design of the famous "Antioch Chalice," dated to the sixth century A.D. The grapevines create a meshlike surface on the chalice. The human figures so carefully arranged within the arbor of grapes reinforced the symbolic meanings ascribed to the vine as a "Tree of Life" – meanings that lie at the heart of Christianity.

By the sixth century A.D. the miracle of the Eucharist was sufficiently understood that the wine vessel for Communion needed not include the grapevine in its decoration; however, the motif persisted in ecclesiastical use, often combining the symbol of the grape (for wine) with that of wheat (for the Communion bread). Interestingly, the paired symbols of grape and wheat are also attributes of Dionysus and Demeter (the Roman Ceres) respectively – the god of viticulture and the goddess of agriculture.

The symbolic meaning of grape and vine took another direction following the conversion of the emperor Constantine to the Christian faith

The Virgin and Child under a Vine Trellis
1509
Hans Burgkmair (1473–1531)
Woodcut, 22.1 × 15.1
The Metropolitan Museum of Art, New York. Harris Brisbane Dick Fund, 1933

The grape arbor under which the figures are placed alludes to the future Passion of the young Christ, expressing the parallel between wine and blood.

The Crucifixion
1497–99
Albrecht Dürer (1471–1528)
Germany
Woodcut, 38.6 × 27.9
Cooper-Hewitt Museum, New
York. Gift of Leo Wallerstein,
1950-5-16

The blood that issues from the
wounds in Christ's hands, feet,
and side is being collected in
chalices held by adoring angels.

kerkē alle moſt wt dē wijnkelre vand' op
ghecruuſt' zidē xpriſti zijn wtgheuloten.
dicim boete tieghen zuyete onſer zonden

comen zonderlinghe om die zondare t
houden · recht als een groot aerſte to zi

in the fourth century A.D. From this date forward, the history of religious power was closely allied to the history of temporal power, and the grape-vine was called into service to lend visual credence to this monumental cultural change.

Justinian, who ruled the Byzantine Empire from A.D. 527 to 565, had already completed the great church of Hagia Sophia (Holy Wisdom) in Constantinople, and bethought himself of the western part of his realm. Rome, already languishing, was too difficult to defend as the capital. Still, Justinian wanted to affirm his presence as emperor on Italian soil. He chose Ravenna, which had only been a port of call for the royal navy on the Adriatic coast, for the new capital that would bear the stamp of his personality.

Ravenna was endowed with three new churches, the most impressive being the royal chapel, San Vitale. On either side of the entrance are two glittering mosaics of multicolored glass chips, hovering between the floor and the galleries, as though between heaven and earth. In one the empress Theodora is shown with her attendants in solemn procession toward the altar. It is the queen herself, not a deacon or a priest, who bears the huge chalice filled with purple wine. Behind her head floats a halo, a visual statement unparalleled, and almost blasphemous, of the appointment of rulers by God. Here the divine right of kings and queens is stated in stunning clarity.

The power of the vine as a symbol of both heavenly and earthly power is seen in its use as a motif familiar in medieval art — the Tree of Jesse. If we think back to Justinian and Theodora, who masked their origins (Theodora was a circus acrobat before becoming empress!) by designating themselves as the anointed, ruling by the will of God, and adopting the nearly immutable stance of those figures in the San Vitale mosaic, we must not forget that the "divine right" was of little help to the barbarian chiefs who fought one another by fair means or foul in the ensuing centuries. Adding to the confusion caused by constant warfare among different tribes, intrafamilial violence could blur the lines of succession. It is no wonder, then, that genealogy became of paramount importance.

In Abbot Suger's famous twelfth-century church of St. Denis was installed a magnificent stained-glass window representing the family tree of Joseph, Christ's father on earth. Here, the ancestry of Jesus is traced, ending with Joseph and Mary. Nobility of lineage was confirmed by this genealogical tree; the line begins with Jesse, the father of David, who, though the youngest of seven sons, was designated to become king. David is always shown above the sleeping Jesse, from whose side the family tree sprouts. All of the figures, between David and an uncrowned Christ at the apex, wear crowns to make it clear that they, too, were kings. Apparently no one found it strange that it was not Mary, who gave birth to the Son of God, but Joseph who was the descendant of kings. A savior was one thing, a king another, and the descent of kings was patrilineal. By the fourteenth century, the Tree of Jesse was represented as a twining grapevine, the distinguished ancestors of Christ encircled by foliage and clusters of fruit. The continuity of the vine itself reasserted the continuity of the heritage.

In addition, the grape and vine could be used for a multitude of variations. The Virgin was shown seated beneath an arbor of grapes, an allusion to the eventual fate of her infant Son. It was Christ who eventually substituted for the harvest itself in the mystical winepress, in which his suffering achieved redemption through the blood extracted in the same manner as the juice of grapes. One of the most compelling of these images appears in a tapestry that shows the infant Christ blessing with one hand while he squeezes a cluster of grapes in the other. The juice from the grapes runs directly into a Communion chalice placed beneath the cluster.

The symbol of the grapevine could even be separated entirely from the sphere of religion, as in a sixteenth-century allegorical representation of Europa. The bejeweled and heavily robed figure holds a scepter of temporal power in her right hand, while in the left she lifts a vine heavy with fruit. That the grapevine shares pride of place with the scepter to denote the all-encompassing power of the West brings us full circle in the history of the vine, from a symbol of the spirit to that of the political body.

On a secular level, the grapevine continued to amuse and delight, with representations of the labors in the vineyard a popular image in illuminated books. Even the putti in the grapevines, an ancient symbol that had served to express the resurrection and continuity of the spirit for both the Romans and the Early Christians, sometimes were converted into monkeys disporting themselves in vines and branches. Coming late in the history of medieval art, such images suggest that these symbols had lost their deeper underpinnings to become the material of objective examination and even humor; one tradition is coming to an end and the stage is set for a new one to begin.

In Italy it had already started to emerge. The tidal waves of bubonic plague that swept Europe in the fourteenth century – believed to have decimated nearly one-third of its population – certainly had the effect of

Angels Harvesting Grapes
c. 1530
Germany
Woodcut, 12 × 7.6
The Seagram Museum, Waterloo, Ontario

The Young Christ
c. 1500
Brussels, Flanders
Tapestry, wool and metal
thread, 64.8×66
Courtesy The Metropolitan Museum of Art, New York. Bequest
of Benjamin Altman, 1913

The Passion of Christ is forecast
in the gesture of squeezing
grapes into a plain drinking cup,
prefiguring the shedding of His
blood through the Crucifixion
and the use of wine in the Communion chalice.

turning people's thoughts to death. It seemed to be an accurate fulfillment of Saint John's prophecy of Armageddon (Revelations 14: 14-20):

> *I looked, and there before me was a white cloud, and seated on it was one "like the son of man" with a crown of gold on his head, and a sharp sickle in his hand. . . . Another angel came out of the temple in heaven, and he too had a sharp sickle. Still another angel who had charge of the fire, came from the altar and called in a loud voice to him who had the sharp sickle, "Take your sharp sickle and gather the clusters of grapes from the earth's vine, because the grapes are ripe." The angel swung his sickle on the earth, gathered its grapes and threw them into the great Winepress of God's wrath. They were trampled in the winepress outside the city [Babylon], and the blood flowed out of the press, rising as high as the horses' bridles. . . .*

For those fortunate few with the economic means to escape the epidemic, retreat to the countryside may have offered more time not only to enjoy the usual entertainments of storyteller, musicians, and the like but also to take a serious interest in the studies of the scholars who were part of their train (if only as scribes). Most of these nobles already knew Church Latin, and now they studied Greek.

A real rage for collecting antique artifacts took hold. Some antique statues in Rome had escaped the idol-destroying phase of early Christianity and the ravages of time. Although these may have been included among the sights for pilgrims who wanted to see the holy places where Saint Peter had preached, there had been no urgency on the part of private patrons to collect statuary from the time of ancient Rome. Suddenly this attitude changed. Not only wealthy citizens but the princes of the Church itself were eager buyers – so eager, in fact, that endless variations on classical themes and figures were supplied to meet the demand.

Some artists were scholars themselves, capable of retranslating ancient myth and legend to meet the needs of a new sophisticated and educated clientele. One such artist was Mantegna, who was uncommonly capable of playing the culture game with his learned patrons. The new patrons appreciated the gods of the ancient world on a more objective level; these gods had become the subject of a collector's catalogue. On the other hand, the works invented by the artists, although very close to the spirit of classical times as well as its forms, often have telltale hints that go beyond the antique: in Mantegna's engraving of a revel, despite the apparent accuracy of every classical pose and detail, one intuits a whole substructure of learned thought not derived from the classics.

Why, one wonders, is the grapevine climbing a fruit tree? Is this the intermingling of the Tree of Knowledge, which caused the downfall of Adam and Eve, combined with the Salvation of the Church? Quite probably; for all their mastery of ancient lore, the nobles had no wish to rebel against a Church whose prelates were as anxious as the lay nobility to study the classics. Rather, an effort to reconcile the two was under way, just as the New Testament in its time honored those prophets of the Old who foretold the coming of the Messiah. The Mantegna print also shows the children, whom we can recognize from many earlier depictions of Bacchus and his followers, to be as drunk as the grown-up satyrs and men. In fact, one detects a faintly moralizing attitude, from the harvesters on the left and the pair drinking on the right to the youth's total loss of sense (or at least rational control) in the middle of the picture.

While putti may help with the harvest in old Roman Bacchic scenes, much as the little boy at the left in Mantegna's print, they are rarely, if ever, shown in a state of total stupor. They may be shown climbing among vines, but never tumbling into a vat. I believe that this, like the Tree of Knowledge embraced by a grapevine, is a Renaissance attempt to keep a sort of balance between good and evil in its enthusiasm for antiquity.

Bacchus
16th century
Venice, Italy
Bronze, height 23.2
The Metropolitan Museum of Art, New York. The Friedsam Collection, The Bequest of Michael Friedsam, 1931

A Bacchanalian Revel
c. 1500
Andrea Mantegna (1431–1506)
Italy
Engraving, 30 × 44.2
Cooper-Hewitt Museum, New
York. Gift of George Campbell
Cooper, 1896-3-4

Allegorical Figure of Europa
c. 1595
Adrien Collaert II (1550–1618),
after Martin de Vos
(1532–1603)
Flanders
Engraving, 21.6 × 25.7
Courtesy The Metropolitan Museum of Art, New York. Gift of
the Estate of James Hazen Hyde,
1959

Wallpaper: "Vine"
Designed 1873
William Morris (1834–1896);
Morris & Co.
Reprinted by Arthur Sanderson
& Sons, Ltd., 1968
England
Paper, 91.5 × 55.4
Cooper-Hewitt Museum, New
York. Gift of Arthur Sanderson
& Sons, Ltd., 1970-1-15A

Vine Pattern with Satyr Family
16th century
School of Albrecht Dürer
Germany
Woodcut, 53.5 × 65.2
Courtesy The Metropolitan Museum of Art, New York. Rogers
Fund, 1922

Bacche pater, prono proſtrati corpore cuncti,
Suppliciter petimus, nobis tua dona ſecundes.

Dona, quibus mæror triſtis, luctuſq; recedit,
Noſtraq; ſollicitis relevantur pectora curis.

C. Schonæus.

The Veneration of Bacchus
1596
Jan Saenredam (1565–1607),
after Hendrick Goltzius
(1558–1617)
Holland
Engraving, 44.2 × 31.4
The Metropolitan Museum of
Art, New York. The Elisha
Whittelsey Collection, The
Elisha Whittelsey Fund, 1951

This representation of Bacchus
transports a classical god into
the midst of a group of humble
sixteenth-century peasants.

Bacchus and Ceres
1810
Felice Giani (1760–1823)
Italy
Pen and brown ink, brown
wash, and graphite, 21.7 × 19.3
Cooper-Hewitt Museum, New
York. Friends of the Museum
Fund, 1901-39-3212

Bacchus, god of viticulture, is
here represented with Ceres,
goddess of agriculture. While
Bacchus is surrounded with
grapes and a wine flagon, Ceres
sits between a sheaf of wheat
and a cornucopia of fruit. The
symbolism of grapes/wine and
wheat/bread continues in Christian art, the two plants sym-
bolizing the elements of the Last
Supper and Communion.

From Mantegna, a great pioneer of the classical revival in the arts of
the region of Venice, the appreciation of antique subjects, myths, and
figures spreads, and the history of Italian art of the subsequent decades is
replete with numerous examples of incidents and stories from the lives of
the gods. Dionysus or Bacchus, while included in the group of the "revived," is no longer a living force in the lives of men.

Images of classical subjects were disseminated to a wide audience
through the medium of prints, which revived the classical gods, goddesses, satyrs, and nymphs in a manner that treats the figures as elements
in an overall pattern. All of the symbols that we expect to find in Bacchic
imagery remain, but here they transmit aesthetic delight rather than phil-
osophical meaning. Other images of Bacchus present the young god as a
mannered and somewhat effeminate figure, surprising the peasantry by
his miraculous appearance in the fields.

The northern part of the Netherlands, which was Protestant, had suf-
fered fiercely under Spain. When it managed to fight its way to freedom,
an explosion of new industries and trade brought comfortable fortunes
to many people. They not only enjoyed their houses, their food and
drink, and the exotic porcelains that came from the Orient, but also to-
bacco from America and wines (which travel well by ship) from France.
All of these served as subject matter for the flourishing art trade. The
Dutch liked pictures of their new-found affluence on the walls of their
homes, as well as maps on which the shipping routes could be traced.
Still, they must have had a superstitious premonition that such good fortune could not be permanent: in the middle of a still life painting showing a panoply of their pleasures, one often finds a skull. Such subjects as
a category are called *Vanitas* pictures, because they remind us of the vain
pleasures of this life. In a sense, they take the other end of the measuring
tape by which we ascertain the value of life.

During the eighteenth century, another period of revival of interest in
the world of the ancients made itself felt throughout the sphere of the

arts. Robert Adam in England did much to restore the graceful harmony of form and ornament that was typical of Roman architecture, particularly after the excavations at Pompeii and Herculaneum in the middle decades of the century had revealed so much of the domestic, rather than the public, life of affluent Roman citizens. Bacchus was, of course, one of the many ancient deities that was revived during the neoclassical period, but more than ever became a decorative allusion to one's knowledge of history. A drawing of Bacchus and Ceres by the Italian artist Felice Gianni shows Bacchus, god of wine, seated next to Ceres, the goddess of wheat. The two elegant creatures appear to be performers in a ballet or tableau. Their godlike powers diminished, they have become a part of the theater of symbols itself and, in one sense, caricatures of their true natures. By the end of the century, Bacchus no longer had the power to impress; he was destined to become the ornamental finial on an elegant porcelain wine barrel. Along with readily available wine, which was

Urn on stand
c. 1748
Modeled by Johann Joachim Kändler (1706–1775); Meissen porcelain factory
Germany
Porcelain, enamel decoration, and gilding, height 53.4
The Antique Porcelain Company, Ltd.

This urn is surmounted by a figure of Bacchus, who holds aloft a drinking glass.

Necklace
c. 1860–70
Castellani
Rome and London
Gold and pearls, length 38
Private collection

Bowl: "Bacchanalian Procession"
Designed 1925
Simon Gate (1883–1945);
Orrefors Glasbruk
Sweden
Blown glass, engraved,
21.5 × 30.5
AB Orrefors Glasbruk, Sweden

being promoted and consumed among a wide sector of the public, the gods themselves had entered the realm of commercial activity.

As is true in many areas of art history, once a symbol has lost its power to affect our lives and our visions, it may return to live a long and healthy life as pattern. The rituals of wine, with their deep-seated and intense cultural meaning, were also subject to this process. By the nineteenth and twentieth centuries, the wine gods and their attributes had become the playthings of connoisseurs; the symbols themselves remained vital only in the lives of the devout.

The only recent instance that I can find of the old religious fervor connected with grapes and wine, whether from pagans or Christians, is in Julia Ward Howe's "Battle Hymn of the Republic": "Mine eyes have seen the glory of the coming of the Lord, He is trampling out the vintage where the grapes of wrath are stored. . . ." We know her source in Saint John's Revelations and the fertile imagery of wine, grape, and the harvest that has survived over the millenniums. As an active Abolitionist, and as an advocate of women's right to vote (which she did not live to see happen), the refrain "His Truth is marching on" takes on new meaning – it is *her* truth that rekindles the flame, and brings the grapevine to life once again.

GEVREY-CHAMBERTIN
Fête du Vin 1925 - Le Roi des Vins "Chambertin"

Celebration and Ceremony:
The Patterns of Ritual

David Revere McFadden

October
From a set of six tapestries of
the zodiac months
c. 1700
Dominique de la Croix;
Gobelins tapestry factory
Paris, France
Tapestry, 345 × 305
Collection Vantage Southeast
Property, Inc., Atlanta, Georgia

This vintage scene includes the
treading of grapes in a large
wooden vat. At the right, a couple is engaged in harvesting fruit
beneath a grape arbor, while another couple in the foreground
samples the wine poured from a
silver flagon into a shallow
bowl.

By the time Euripides wrote of "lovely wine by which our suffering is
stopped," the grape and its intoxicating derivative had already insinuated
themselves into the very core of culture. Not only had wine been accorded a place within the gustatory rituals of our ancestors, it had assumed a central role in the theater of symbolism; the seasonal abundance
of the plant was a living parallel to the concept of regeneration. All of the
activities essential to the nurturing of the grape and the production of
wine, from the pruning and harvesting in the vineyards to the treading of
the fruit, and, above all, its magical transformation into wine, took on an
importance and significance that can be glimpsed not only in the literature that has survived to our own day but also in the thousands of
objects created for the service, enjoyment, and ritual use of wine in ancient cultures.

It should not be surprising that the history of the vine and its wines has
had a dramatic parallel in the story of design and the decorative arts, but
it is easy to overlook the fact that the simple wineglass and bottle from
which we enjoy a glass of wine are linked in purpose and in time to the
origins of viticulture itself. Time is both an aid and an impediment to
understanding that history: an aid because we gain a sense of perspective
on our own past, and an impediment since we can appreciate the design
history of wine only from those relatively few objects from earlier millenniums that have survived into our own day. It is difficult to comprehend
the sheer numbers of drinking vessels, jugs, flagons, and ewers, storage
containers and bottles, and other wine-related objects that have been destroyed and lost through the centuries.

How many wine amphorae were smashed on their way from storage
cellar to serving room, or consigned to an undersea grave as a result of a
storm at sea? About three dozen such jars were miraculously preserved in
King Tut's tomb, intended solely for his use in the afterlife, and the excavations at sites such as Gaza have revealed the immensity of the wine
trade in the ancient world. How many thousands of eighteenth-century
wineglasses, sparkling with refracted light, were sacrificed accidentally or
intentionally at late-night drinking bouts in England through overzealous
toasting? And how many more glasses have met an untimely demise at
the hands of the clumsy or careless? How many gloriously wrought wine
cups and chalices of silver and gold have been stolen and melted for their
metal, or consigned to the silversmith's melting pot simply because they
were no longer "in the fashion"? Although we may never know the figures, the astonishing number of vessels that have followed the rule of
"the survival of the fittest" cannot but impress us, and they emphasize
the importance of wine as a stimulus to design and craftsmanship.

Wine has been espoused as the inspiration of countless poets and artists, but its influence has been felt in nearly all of the arts, from architecture to decorative arts and industrial design. Wine has served as a link
between the realm of the flesh and that of the spirit. It has contributed to
the growth of science and technology, has affected national and international economies and trade, has influenced the growth of cities, and has

Serving Wine
From Petrus de Crescentius,
*Vom Ackerbaw, Erdtwucher,
und Bawleüte . . .* , Strasbourg,
1531
Woodcut, with hand coloring,
27 × 18
Smithsonian Institution Libraries, Washington, D.C.

Glass
c. 1785–90
Holland
Glass, stippled design, 15.9 × 6.3
The Metropolitan Museum of
Art, New York. The Munsey
Fund, 1927

Inscribed in Dutch with the
phrase, "Our brotherhood shall
never abate," this glass is stippled with two figures acknowl-
edging a toast of friendship.

**The Brothers Clarke with Other
Gentlemen Taking Wine**
c. 1730–35
Gawen Hamilton
(c. 1697–1737)
England
Oil on canvas, 82.5 × 115.5
Yale Center for British Art, New
Haven, Connecticut. Paul
Mellon Collection

This typical mid-eighteenth-cen-
tury group portrait shows the elegant gentlemen seated around a
covered table furnished with
dark-green glass decanter bottles
and a clear glass carafe. The
glasses used for drinking are of a
familiar tapered, conical shape.
Of added interest is the servant
at left, placing decanter bottles
in a large wine cooler on the
floor. On the sideboard or buffet
at left can be seen a two-handled
ceremonial drinking cup.

Drinking glasses
18th–20th century
Cooper-Hewitt Museum, New
York

From left to right: Sweden, c.
1980; probably Austria, c. 1900;
Switzerland, 18th century; Germany, 18th century; United
States, Tiffany Studios, early
20th century; England, 18th century; England or Ireland, late
18th–early 19th century; probably Austria, c. 1900; Finland, c.
1978; Italy, Salviati, c. 1920.

helped to shape landscapes. Wine has highlighted our religious beliefs and our recreations, has served sacred and secular ends, and has given us both reasons and means for celebration. Viewed from the perspective of over five thousand years of history, the design of wine-related objects and implements reflects at the same time the continuity of our cultures and the monumental changes that have occurred.

The basic nature of grape-growing and wine-making, being cyclical and seasonal, and the social and religious contexts in which wine has been used have inseparably allied the process and the product to ritual over the thousands of years since the fortuitous discovery of the drink. The grape, along with its family of fermented and distilled beverages, has been as tenacious and abundant a force in our cultures as the roots and tendrils of the plant itself. In ritual and religious settings, whether as a libation poured over the grave of an ancestor or hero, in its use for the kiddush, or in its sanctification in the Eucharist, wine has been clearly accorded a place of honor and status. On a secular plane, the imbibing of wine is commonplace at ritual events such as anniversaries, birthdays, and weddings, and we can also recognize the subtle rituals of behavior played out at a simple dinner party.

Ritual, whether sacred or secular, depends on two elements: recognizable and acceptable actions that carry meaning (such as the "toast"), and actions that maintain their meaning over time through repetition (as in the rites of the Mass). The choreography of ritual is readily apparent in

Wall painting
Showing garden with grapevines around a pool
From the tomb of Kenamun (No. 93)
Reign of Amenhotep II, 1424–1417 B.C.
Thebes, Egypt
Redrawn by Leonard H. Lesko
From Norman de Garis Davies, *The Tomb of Ken-Amun at Thebes*, I, New York, 1930, plate 47

Set of tiles
Representing grapes and lotus
Probably Dynasty XX, reign of Ramses III, 1198–1166 B.C.
Egypt
Faience, 7.1 × 29.1
The Brooklyn Museum, New York. Charles Edwin Wilbour Fund

religion, where the repetition of action renews its meaning each time it
occurs. For instance, the breaking of a wineglass at a Jewish wedding
symbolizes fulfillment along with a reminder that happiness must be tem-
pered with the knowledge that sorrow is unavoidable. But does such ritual continue to play a role in our everyday lives? One need only recall, I
think, the deep-seated emotions that combine reflection and anticipation
released by the uncorking of a bottle of Champagne on New Year's Eve,
or the feeling of welcome that is provided by the sharing of wine at
dinner among friends or associates. Even these familiar pleasures are, to
a great extent, ritualized expressions of culture; time, setting, season, and
ceremony are vital to the patterns of these rituals. As one examines the
design history of wine, including the tools and techniques of the vintner
and the personal necessities and paraphernalia of the wine-drinker, it becomes apparent that the history of design and the history of wine cannot
be easily separated.

The most dramatic and obvious example of continuity and change is to
be found in the architecture of the vineyard itself. In Egypt, the hiero-
glyphic sign for *vine* was compounded in the words meaning *gardener*
and *orchard*, delineating its central role as a meaningful idea, and it is
from Egypt that we have some of the clearest indications of the stress
placed on the design of the vineyard itself. Egyptian wall paintings such
as those from Thebes provide confirmation of the status of the vineyard;
a schematic ground plan of a vineyard often shows the vines within a
garden complex that includes palm trees and pools inhabited by aquatic
birds. Such gardens were intended to provide visual pleasure as well as
efficient protection and irrigation of the prized vines, and the vineyard
was seen as an extension of royal prerogative. Egyptian vines were often
trained to grow in trellised rows or arbors beneath which servants could
tend and harvest the bounty. The ancestors of all later vineyard designs,
they illustrate the combination of visual and practical requirements.

Vine arbors were not, of course, the only system available for training
the vine, although the practice has survived in household vineyards in
areas such as southern Italy and Sicily. By the sixteenth century A.D.,
many other systems had been adopted to maximize the productivity of
the vine; a print issued in Strasbourg in the beginning of that century
serves conveniently as a catalogue of the vine systems employed since the

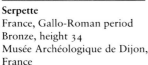

Serpette
France, Gallo-Roman period
Bronze, height 34
Musée Archéologique de Dijon,
France

days of the ancients. Certain of the vines are being grown directly upon a neighboring tree, which must be among the oldest of systems. Other vines have been trained to provide an attractive pergola beneath which one could walk, recalling the arbors of the Egyptians. A variation on the pergola is the *vinea camerata,* a geometric framework that supports the vines in an orderly fashion and facilitates the pruning of the vines to a controllable height.

The last of the systems depicted is undoubtedly the most important for later winegrowers: staked vines on the hillside, planted far enough apart to permit workers to tend, prune, and harvest, set the stage for the modern vineyard arranged in rows across the landscape. Besides assuring an even supply of sunlight and ease of maintenance, this system has proven adaptable to modern mechanized harvesting. Technology and wine-making have gone hand in hand over the centuries, although the most radical developments seem to have occurred within the past century. The appearance of a metal monster looming over the vines removes most of the romance of the old-fashioned (and backbreaking) hand-harvesting of the grapes, but wine, too, has had to face the Industrial Revolution, which affected all aspects of viticulture from planting to the bottling and drinking of wine.

In addition to convenient row systems for grape-growing, many landscapes demanded clever and competent engineering to adjust to difficult terrains. The topography of the Sonoma Valley in California is determined by the vine in the same way that that of sixteenth-century Germany was, with its cities set as jewels in verdant vineyards. Few who have visited wine districts in the Rhine Valley, Switzerland, or southern Italy can easily forget the dramatic impact of terraced vineyards that rise from the lowlands into the clouds.

Like the vineyard itself, tools and equipment used in the growing of grapes have both a functional and symbolic design history. Specialized implements for the pruning of the vine and the harvesting of grapes were developed in the ancient world, and none expresses the continuity of design with more elegance and simplicity than the *serpette,* the symbolic attribute of vintners over the centuries. This small knife sports a curved blade that provides a curved extension to the hand and wrist, permitting

Serpettes and clippers
19th and 20th centuries
Switzerland
Wood and metal
Musée Vaudois de la Vigne et du
Vin, Aigle, Switzerland

The *serpette* was an essential
hand tool for the grape-grower,
providing an efficient cutting
blade to prune the vines and to
harvest the grapes. The form of
the knife changed little from the
Roman period until the nineteenth century, when it was supplanted in popularity by the
crossed-blade clipper. This tool,
too, was superseded by mechanized grape harvesters. Pruning,
a skill involving human judg-
ment, still requires careful hand-
work.

Habit de Vigneron

the user to make a clean and efficient cut through a branch for either pruning or harvesting. Extensively used in the Roman period, such knives have been found in Roman outposts throughout Europe. The *serpette* served its purpose with grace and elegance for over fifteen hundred years, until it was supplanted by the scissors-like clipper introduced in the last century; like so many other tools and techniques common to the vineyard, the *serpette* was rendered obsolete nearly overnight in the wake of nineteenth-century innovation.

A similar design history, with obvious variations, can be traced in objects as humble and as essential as the basket used for collecting grapes at harvest time. Ancient Roman reliefs depict the transporting of grapes from vineyard to the treading vat in woven reed baskets whose forms remained virtually unchanged until this century. Each region of grape-growers developed preferred forms for these baskets, and one can recognize in illuminated manuscripts the ancestors of the double-bodied shoulder basket of Burgundy and the tapered conical *hotte* common to French vineyards from Champagne to Bordeaux. Now generally relegated to the walls of collectors of wine memorabilia, the traditional basket has been replaced by modern plastic or the machine.

The history of design for wine is written in the specialized equipment necessitated by the treading and pressing of the grapes to produce the

Man harvesting grapes
c. 1950
Courtesy Conseil Régional de
Bourgogne, Dijon, France

The harvester is using a typical
Côte de Beaune double basket,
which, when filled, can be easily
supported on the shoulder.

Basket
Used for the grape harvest
Late 19th–early 20th century
Berry, France
Wicker
Musée National des Arts et Tra-
ditions Populaires, Paris

Basket
Used for the grape harvest
1859
Yvorne, Switzerland
Wood, capacity 45 liters
Musée Vaudois de la Vigne et du
Vin, Aigle, Switzerland

Harvesting machine
20th century
Courtesy JAs Hennessy & Co.,
Cognac, France

The Industrial Revolution,
which began to make itself felt
during the nineteenth century in
the wine industry, has resulted
in mechanized replacements for
hand labor in the vineyard.

Relief
With wine-pressing scene
Detail of east wall of the tomb
of Puimra
Reign of Hatshepsut,
1503–1482 B.C.
Thebes, Egypt
Photograph by The Egyptian Expedition, The Metropolitan Museum of Art; Courtesy The
Metropolitan Museum of Art,
New York

The relief shows the pressing of
grapes in a linen sack press; two
workers are shown applying
pressure to the twisted linen bag
filled with grapes by using long
wooden poles. The juice from
the grapes flows in a steady
stream from the sack into a re-
ceptacle placed on the ground.

liquid from which the wine will be fermented. Treading the grapes using
only the weight and energy of the human body ranks among the oldest
and most romanticized methods of extracting the vital fluid from the ripe
grapes. This time-honored tradition, ousted more efficiently by technology than by modern phobias about hygiene, assumed a mystical and
symbolic meaning early in the history of viticulture. Familiar to us are
the words of Isaiah, "I will tread them in mine anger and trample them in
my fury," in which the trodden grapes serve as symbolic substitutes for
the enemies of the Lord.

The treading of grapes proceeds to another stage of technology – that
of pressing the grapes in a mechanical device. It is known from wall
paintings that the Egyptians made extensive use of a linen "bag" press, in
which the crushed grapes were twisted in a fabric envelope between two
upright posts. This was superseded by the more efficient and powerful
wooden torque or screw press, which remained in general use until the
development of iron screw presses. Today, a stainless steel and plastic air-
compression system performs this task.

The growing of grapes and the pressing of the fruit is but a part of the
narrative of wine history and design. After the fermentation of the grape
juice, it was necessary to store the wine for future use. From the earliest
days of viticulture, it was essential to provide secure vessels for wine
storage, not, as we may generally assume today, to allow the contents to

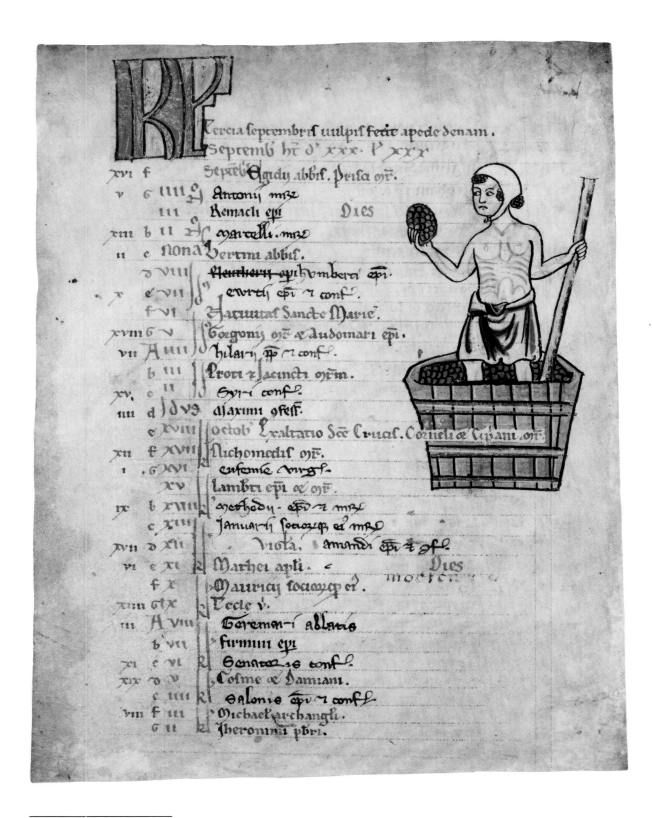

Tercia septembris uulpis ferit a pede denam.
Septembs ht d xxx P xxx

xvi	f		Septeb Agidii abbis. Prisca oir.	
v	g	iiii	Antonii mr̄	
		iii	Remacli epi	Dies
xiii	b	ii	Marcelli mr̄	
ii	c	Nona	Bertini abbis.	
	d	viii	Eleutherii epi Lumberti epi	
x	e	vii	ewrth epi ⁊ conf.	
	f	vi	Natiuitas Sancte Marie.	
xviii	g	v	Gorgonii oir ⁊ Audomari epi.	
vii	A	iiii	hilarii pp ⁊ conf.	
	b	iii	Proti ⁊ Iacincti oir̄m.	
xv	c	ii	Syri conf.	
iiii	d	Idus	Maximi oisess.	
	e	xviii	octob Exaltatio Scē Cruas. Cornelii ⁊ Cipani. oir.	
xii	f	xvii	Nichomedis oir.	
i	g	xvi	Eufemie uirḡs.	
		xv	lamberti epi ⁊ oir.	
ix	b	xiiii	Methodii epi ⁊ mr̄	
	c	xiii	Ianuarii sociozoq ei mr̄	
xvii	d	xii	Viola. amandi epi ⁊ cf.	
vi	e	xi	Mathei apli.	Dies
	f	x	Mauricii sociozoq ei.	mortei
xiiii	g	ix	Tecle v.	
iii	A	viii	Soremari abbatis	
	b	vii	firmini epi	
xi	c	vi	Senatoris conf.	
xix	d	v	Cosme ⁊ Damiani.	
	e	iiii	Salonis epi ⁊ conf.	
viii	f	iii	Michael archangli.	
	g	ii	Iheronimi pbri.	

September
Calendar leaf in Latin
Mid-13th century
Flanders
Manuscript on vellum,
20.3 × 15.2
The Pierpont Morgan Library,
New York. M. 908, folio 4

87

Double-screw winepress
17th–18th century
Aube region, France
Wood and metal,
182 × 195 × 167
Musée des Pressoirs, Mercier
Champagne, Epernay, France

Winepress
From Denis Diderot, *Encyclopédie*, vol. 1, *Recueil de Planches sur les Sciences, les Arts Libéraux et les Arts Méchaniques avec leur explication*, Paris, 1762
Engraving, 39 × 49.8
Cooper-Hewitt Museum Library, New York

The grandest of designs for winepresses included in Diderot's *Encyclopédie*, this gigantic machine, made up of two presses side by side, was apparently made to be operated by one man. Whether ever realized or not, it was conceived as a great labor-saving system.

Wine-pressing
Early 20th century
Courtesy JAs Hennessy & Co.,
Cognac, France

Air-compression press
20th century
Courtesy Simi Winery, California

The technology of wine-pressing
has developed rapidly since the
nineteenth century. The wooden
screw press used in the ancient
world continued with relatively
few changes until the last century, when metal parts replaced
many of the wooden compo-
nents of the press. In this century, the air-compression
press—fast, efficient, and easily
controlled—has gained popularity among wine producers.

age, but to protect the sensitive liquid from air that would convert wine
into undesirable amounts of vinegar, thus assuring its availability during
the long months between harvests.

The wine bottles so familiar to us today are comparatively recent arriv-
als on the scene. Storage of wines in the ancient world was virtually
dependent upon the skills of the potter who fashioned capacious
amphorae of unglazed clay for both the storage and shipping of wine.
The clay body protected the wine from light and heat; with an inner
coating of pitch or resin, it was also a fairly efficient barrier against evap-

oration. Such amphorae were commonplace storage vessels, and although many were. undoubtedly employed for the storage of oil or other comestibles, certain of the vessels used in Egypt and Rome carried a stamp to indicate the contents. Handle shards found in the palace of Amenhotep III of Egypt included information about the quantity of wine within, the name of the wine-maker, and the intended purpose of the wine – e.g., "for offerings." The simple expedient of marking the wine jars must be acknowledged as the great-grandparent of the modern paper label.

The use of ceramic storage vessels for wine held sway in the wine-producing areas of southern Europe, while in more northerly climes the wooden cask or barrel gained early and long-lasting acceptance. Arising from the ample supply of wood in the verdant forests of the north, the wooden cask was also a logical development of the region's wood-based craft. The cooper was accorded especial prominence in areas such as Germany and France; even Roman reliefs show the transporting of wine from northern centers in large barrels. The oak used in the manufacturing of casks, barrels, and tuns imparted a special flavor to the contents, an effect used to advantage when the medieval art of distillation was applied to wines to create eau-de-vie, brandy, cognac, and armagnac, and to satisfy a later demand for aged wines. Whereas the production of ceramic amphorae for wine storage declined dramatically with the introduction of the glass bottle for holding and aging wine, the traditional oak barrel still remains without peer in the world of modern technology, and the craft of coopering continues to be practiced with few changes in the *tonnelleries* of master craftsmen It is worth noting that the process of converting oak staves into a curved barrel depends upon a technology that precedes by centuries the introduction of bentwood for furniture.

Wine, of course, was not consumed directly from its storage container, whether ceramic or wooden, but was transferred to other vessels in small quantities. From the earliest days of wine consumption, considerable ceremony and no little expense surrounded the presentation of wine at table. In Egypt, wine amphorae carried from the cellar were sometimes

Cooper Making Tubs and Baskets
From Petrus de Crescentius, *Vom Ackerbow, Erdtwucher, und Bawleüte . . .* , Strasbourg, 1531
Woodcut, with hand coloring, 27 × 18
Smithsonian Institution Libraries, Washington, D.C.

Cooper in the Tonnellerie Taransaud
c. 1980
Cognac, France
Courtesy JAs Hennessy & Co., Cognac, France

Stamped amphora
Two-handled storage jar
c. 100 B.C.
Rhodes, Greece
Pottery, 82 × 33
The University Museum, University of Pennsylvania, Philadelphia

Amphora handles
Rhodes, Greece, Hellenistic period
Pottery, lengths 11.5 and 8.5
The University Museum, University of Pennsylvania, Philadelphia

The handles show their makers' marks, which, in combination with the stamp of an authorizing official, attested to the capacity of the amphora.

Column krater
Showing satyrs making wine
c. 460 B.C.
Attributed to the Cleveland Painter
Greece, Attic
Pottery, red-figured decoration, 32.5 × 26.5
The Metropolitan Museum of Art, New York. Rogers Fund, 1941

The satyrs, dressed in leopard skins, are treading grapes in a raised trough with a lip that causes the juice to run into a tub underneath.

**Family of the Basel Guild
Master Hans Rudolf Faesch**
1559
Hans Hug Kluber
(1535/6–1578)
Basel, Switzerland
Tempera on canvas,
127.5 × 207.5
Courtesy Kunstmuseum Basel

This family portrait shows many
of the types of drinking vessels
used in the homes of the well-to-
do. On the table are a number of
footed beakers. The patriarch of
the family is drinking from an
elaborate standing cup with a
highly embossed surface. A
small flagon rests on the table,
while larger flagons and flasks
are being chilled in the wine
cooler in front of the table.

Wine cooler
c. 1775
England
Mahogany, brass, and gilt
bronze, 63.5 × 72.4 × 52
The Metropolitan Museum of
Art, New York. Untermyer Col-
lection, 1964

Cellarette
c. 1815–20
Philadelphia, Pennsylvania
Mahogany, 73.5 × 72 × 58.2
Philadelphia Museum of Art.
Given in Memory of Caroline S.
Gratz, by Simon Gratz

provided with ornamental collars of flowers as a part of the ritual of service. In ancient Greece, some of the most magnificent and imposing of vessels – the *kraters* – were reserved for the mixing of wine and water, as was the custom. An additional refinement for Greek imbibers came in the form of the *psykter*, or wine cooler, from which the refreshing and inebriating liquid was ladled into a variety of vessels.

In the Middle Ages, the presentation of wine at a banquet or meal was a duty and honor reserved for upper-echelon servants; the proud aloofness of many a present-day wine steward is a dim reminder of this role. Serving vessels included the flagon and ewer, fashioned of costly precious materials such as silver or gold or of finely painted ceramics. Generally, the drinking vessels of guests at a medieval feast were filled away from the table, presented for drinking, and removed until the next draught was called for. In illustrations from manuscripts and late medieval woodcuts that narrate the meals of worthies, there is seldom (if ever) a cup for each guest; host and guests of honor were served from the most impressive and important vessel, while other guests shared cups and goblets. (The "set" of matched drinking vessels, an idea that has been with us for little more than two hundred years, would have been a bizarre aberration at a medieval feast.) Probably the most impressive of objects designed specifically for the service of wine at this period was the massive and imposing wine cooler. Made in considerable numbers from the late medieval period through the early decades of the eighteenth century, these handy table-side refrigerators held cold or iced water and any number of wine ewers, flagons, or jugs. It was common to have wine brought from cellar storage to table in portable vessels, from which it could be parceled out among the guests, and the wine cooler provided a suitable holding area between servings.

The wine cooler survived into the eighteenth century in its massive form, but by the second half of the century it was reduced to the smaller tabletop wine cooler. While no less grand in materials and execution, this held only a single bottle of wine in readiness. Wine coolers for domestic use peaked in their popularity in the early decades of the nineteenth century, when silversmiths such as Paul Storr created some of the more opulent examples, but even table-side versions have remained in use today for serving white wine and Champagne in restaurants, where they provide an effective barrier to movement for diners and waiters alike.

For wines that did not require cooling, the eighteenth century also saw the rise to popularity of the wine "slide," known most often as a "coaster." Originally coasters served to facilitate the passing of wine from one man to another; bottles were brought out for serious drinking during the eighteenth and early nineteenth centuries only after the women had been dismissed to the drawing room and the table cleared of its covering and impedimenta. Most coasters were constructed of a smoothly polished wooden or fabric-covered plinth that glided across the table without scratching the exposed mahogany surface and were fitted with a gallery (often of silver) that stabilized the bottle while in transit. In this more relaxed atmosphere servants generally were not required to stand in readiness, and bottles that could be "coasted" from one person to another were ideal. The wine coaster survives as a component of dining ritual today. When it became commonplace to leave a covering on the

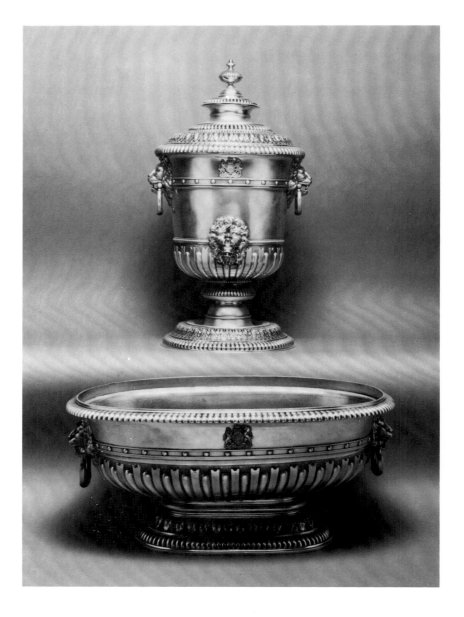

Abr. Drentwett Sen. inv. et del.

G. Heinr. Schifflin Sculps.

Cum Privil. Sac. Cæs. Maj.

ÆSTAS.

Ieremias Wolff excud. Aug.Vind.

table throughout the meal, the coaster shifted from a convenience to movement to a simple protective device against wine spills on the linen.

The social rituals of wine drinking, of which only a few have been mentioned, were dramatically altered by the general acceptance of the wine bottle, used for both the storage and serving of wine. By the seventeenth century, glassmakers in England had developed a dark-colored glass bottle for beer. This bottle included a raised flange at the neck opening that permitted a cork or stopper to be tied in place to protect the contents. By 1681, a "Steel Worme" for extracting the corks from bottles was recorded; the fortuitous pairing of bottle and cork had, as its offspring, the corkscrew.

Although glass vessels had been used in earlier days to transport wine from storage cellar or cask to table, the bottles that came into more general use at the end of the seventeenth century served quite a different purpose; wine that had gone through its first fermentation could be bottled, corked, and stored for aging. The wine thus was able to mature in a single container. Glass, being impervious, prevented contact with destructive oxygen, halted evaporation of the contents, eradicated tainting of the flavor of the wine through contact with foreign substances, and – an important factor – protected the contents from exposure to light, due to its dense coloration. It is certainly no accident that the development of Champagne in the second half of the seventeenth century in the laboratory and cellar of Dom Pérignon occurred at the same time as the perfection of the glass storage bottle, since the *méthode champenoise* requires that a second fermentation of the wine occur inside the bottle itself.

During the course of the eighteenth century the bottle underwent a metamorphosis from a squat rounded body with a straight upright neck to the cylindrical form that we know today, which can be easily stored on the horizontal. This prevented the cork from drying out and exposing the wine to the air. Other details of bottle design are worth noting: the

Coaster wagon
1828
Benjamin Smith (1793–1850)
London, England
Silver-gilt and wood, 12.7 × 48.2
Collection Harveys of Bristol, England

An innovative refinement in wine service was the wine wagon, which permitted decanters of wine to be moved easily from one person to the next at table.

Pair of wine coasters
1814
Paul Storr (1771–1844)
London, England
Silver-gilt and mahogany,
8.9 × 15
Collection Simone and Alan
Hartman

**Sceau à bouteille
(Bottle cooler)**
One of a pair
1792
Jean-Jacques Dieu, after models
by Jean-Claude Duplessis (d.
1774); Sèvres porcelain factory
France
Hard-paste porcelain,
16.5 × 24.1
The J. Paul Getty Museum, Mal-
ibu, California

These coolers, each designed to
hold a single decanter bottle or
carafe of wine, are decorated
with gold and platinum over a
black ground to simulate Orien-
tal lacquer.

Claret jug: "Vintage" ewer
1854
Joseph Angell III
(c. 1816–c. 1891)
London, England
Silver-gilt, 31.5 × 12.5
Cooper-Hewitt Museum, New
York. Gift of Miss Louise B.
Scott, 1936-21-1

This ewer design was created for
the 1851 Crystal Palace exhibition. The ornamentation consists
of a network of trellised grapevines being harvested by putti.

Decanter
1865–66
Designed by William Burges
(1827–1881) for James Nicholson;
maker's mark of Richard Green
England
Glass, silver, gems, malachite,
and rock crystal, height 29.5
Victoria and Albert Museum,
London

Wine jug
1580–90
Factory of Master Anno
Knutgen
Siegburg, Germany
Salt-glazed stoneware and tin,
height 29.2
Museum of Fine Arts, Boston.
Gift of R. Thornton Wilson in
memory of Florence Ellsworth
Wilson

Decanters and glasses
Designed 1983
Vittorio Rigattieri; Cenedese &
Albarelli
Murano, Italy
Glass, decanter: height 28; flute:
height 12.5
Cooper-Hewitt Museum, New
York. Gift of Cenedese & Al-
barelli

Corkscrew
1985
Italy
Plastic and metal, length 11
Courtesy Wine Research Group,
New York

familiar "kick," or raised portion of the underside of most wine bottles, probably originated as a simple expedient to prevent the rough "pontil" mark – the remnants of the blob of glass that held the bottle in place while being worked and shaped – from scratching the surface of a table. With the introduction of mold-blown bottles that could be produced rapidly and of consistent size and volume, the kick remained, presumably to add stability to the bottle when upright. The kick had quite a different reason for being retained in the production of Champagne: since Champagne undergoes a second fermentation in the bottle, considerable pressure is built up inside the fragile glass body wall. The high kick allowed for a more even distribution of pressure inside the bottle, preventing disastrous explosions (which seemed to have been a serious problem for early Champagne makers such as Dom Pérignon). For the same reason, Champagne bottles are much thicker than those of their more quiescent sister wines. In wine history, one good idea spawns another; soon after the revolution in bottling occurred, the wine rack and bin that we know today emerged as essential equipment for any wine collector.

The English glassmakers led the way in the production of glass wine bottles, but by the nineteenth century, glasshouses throughout Europe were producing their own distinctive variations on the form. Bottle shapes became a part of the identifying "signature" of a specific wine or the wine of a region. Today, one can recognize the slope-shouldered bottle of Burgundy, the straight-sided cylinder of Bordeaux, or the tall and svelte bottle of the Rhine area, each with its own color as well as shape. Even in our own century, there have been efforts to create memorable bottles as a part of the international marketing of wine.

Wines that are aged in bottle will often cast off a sediment that can be most efficiently removed by decanting. In the nineteenth century, it would be rare to encounter any wine served from the bottle in which it was stored; decanting was considered not only a necessary kindness to

Wine bottles
18th century
England
Blown glass
The Corning Museum of Glass,
Corning, New York

These three bottles illustrate major types of wine bottles used during the eighteenth century. At left a bottle of c. 1710–20, with a flattened globular body (height 14 cm); center, a bottle of c. 1756, with a more compact and straight-sided profile, bearing a stamp "J. Dason 1756" (23.2 cm); and, at right, a bottle of c. 1780–90, with a shape similar to that of the modern wine bottle (29.2 cm).

good wine but an essential decorum. Wine decanters in many forms proliferated, many made *en suite* with the glassware to be used for its consumption. The decanter joined the growing number of tabletop accouterments of the nineteenth century.

The use of standard bottles and the process of decanting wines prior to use had two other dramatic effects on the history of wine-related design. By the late eighteenth or early nineteenth century, paper labels were used to identify the contents of some types of wine. Quite simple and generic, these labels simply told the potential consumer what to expect inside, giving little information about the specifics of production. By comparison, the Egyptian stamped bottles were extremely informative. However, by the nineteenth century, more information was required, and as the marketing of wines became a more competitive process, individual vineyards created their own distinctive signature labels. Wines that had been decanted for table use also required identification, and the most elegant version of the wine label – the "bottle ticket" – gained general acceptance in the late eighteenth and early nineteenth centuries.

The bottle ticket, a small sign suspended by a chain that fit conveniently over the neck of a decanter, was inscribed or enameled with a generic designation such as "Mountain," "Madeira," or "Claret." Silver or silver-gilt were the favored materials for bottle tickets, which often became vehicles for fine craftsmanship. Within the course of the nineteenth century, the paper label grew in importance while the bottle ticket faded into antiquarian oblivion. To a great extent, the label on modern

wine bottles is the most obvious holdover from the grander years of elegant presentation of wines, and wine producers have not lost an opportu-
nity to attract a buyer through impressive graphic designs for labels and
other promotional materials.

Wine-drinking has been surrounded with paraphernalia since its earliest days, and many of the rituals of wine consumption are still dependent upon small but elegant refinements. The ancient Greeks were served
their wine from silver ladles, and for ancient Romans, the sediment or
lees from a portion of wine could be extracted with an elegant pierced
bronze strainer. Funnels provided an efficient means of transferring wine
from one container to another, and Roman examples made of blown
glass are known. With the eighteenth-century practice of decanting came
the need for silver funnels and siphons, while quantities of wine, mea-
sured in a glass or metal *modiolus* in the ancient world, continue to be
reckoned in carefully graduated carafes of varying sizes. Corkscrews have
never faded from the armament of the dedicated wine-drinker since their
appearance in the seventeenth century, and each year sees the addition of
many new designs and materials to the family of cork extractors.

Other traditions seem to have faded away with time; in the eighteenth
century it was common to make wineglasses available at table in company with a wineglass rinser or glass cooler. Individual coolers and
rinsers, sometimes referred to as "wash glasses," could be used for rinsing the wineglass between servings. The glass wash basin made an elegant addition to any table; in 1759, George Washington ordered a set
from a London merchant.

The grandest of wineglass coolers, however, are the monteiths that became popular in England around the beginning of the eighteenth century.
The monteith was a capacious bowl with a scalloped or notched rim that

permitted a number of wineglasses to be held upside down by the flattened circular foot, the rims submerged in chilled water. Although the majority of monteiths that survive today are made of silver, glass examples are not unknown. Many of the silver versions have a removable notched collar that converts the monteith into a punch bowl, while others made of porcelain, most notably those produced at the Sèvres factory in France, were clearly intended to serve solely for the elegant ritual of wineglass presentation.

The celebrations and ceremonies of wine, recorded in the panoply of designs and decorative objects created for its service and enjoyment, find a central focus in the vessels from which wine is consumed. It is easy for us to take the widely available common wineglass, whether the transparent half-bubble of glass on an elongated stem or the sturdy and serviceable beaker, for granted. Yet this object is one of the most direct and dramatic links between wine-drinking today and the origins of wine itself. Wine vessels – bowls, beakers, goblets, chalices, flutes, tazzas, and cups – have figured significantly in the social and cultural patterns of wine-drinking, and play prominent roles in the rituals that have been created and maintained for centuries.

Wine utensils
18th and 19th centuries
Silver, silver-gilt, and steel
Courtesy Duane Voth, New
York

The paraphernalia that sur-
rounds the drinking of wine today—temperature gauges, digital
vintage charts, and instant wine-
breathers—has its ancestry in the
elegant accouterments that wine
enthusiasts have always prized.

Wine bottles
20th century
Europe and America
Glass
Courtesy Wine Research Group,
New York

Since the development of the
wine bottle as a standard storage
vessel for wines in the eighteenth
century, a tremendous variety of
forms has emerged to indicate
the contents. Although many
bottle types are promotional
novelties, others carry significant
information in their shape,
color, and capacity. Included in
this group are many standard
bottle shapes from Germany,
France, the United States, Italy,
Portugal, and Spain, their na-
tionalities and contents confirmed by the design.

Mechanical decanting cradle
1830–48
Christofle
Paris, France
Silver, 38 × 38
Christofle, Orfèvre à Paris

Innovative designs of the nineteenth century included the mechanical decanting cradle. With this device, a bottle of wine could be decanted without risk of disturbing the sediment.

Verrière
(Glass cooler)
1772
Sèvres porcelain factory
France
Soft-paste porcelain, 12.2 × 29.9
Cooper-Hewitt Museum, New
York. Gift of the Estate of
Charles Sampson; The Charles
Sampson Memorial Fund,
1977-57-1

Drawing for a verrière
Jacques Micaud (active
1757–1810)
France
Pen and ink and watercolor,
27.2 × 41.6
Cooper-Hewitt Museum, New
York. Friends of the Museum
Fund, 1938-88-8316

"Wash Glass" basin
Late 18th century
England
Glass, cut and engraved,
8.6 × 14.6
Cooper-Hewitt Museum, New
York. Gift of Mr. and Mrs.
Arthur Wiesenberger,
1968-160-3

Small glass bowls for rinsing a
wineglass were popular addi-
tions to the tabletop in the late
eighteenth century.

Dessiné par J.M. Moreau le Jeune.   Gravé par Helman 1781

Le Souper Fin
1781
Isidor Helman, after Jean-
Michel Moreau le Jeune
(1741–1814)
France
Engraving, 38.3 × 30.5
The Metropolitan Museum of
Art, New York. Purchase, 1934

The merry diners at this late-
night repast are drinking wine
that has been chilled in the built-
in cooling chambers of the table-
side stands. Their glasses have
been rinsed and cooled in the
small porcelain verrière sitting
on the upper platform of the
stand.

Bowl
Late 5th century B.C.
Tell el-Maskhuta, Egypt
Silver, cast, 7.8 × 17.2
The Brooklyn Museum, New
York. Charles Edwin Wilbour
Fund

All drinking vessels derived from practical forms with a basic purpose – to convey liquid from hand to mouth. One may posit the origins of man-made vessels in natural forms that have been recognized as useful. The cupped hands, the bowl formed by a split gourd, the horn of an animal, a shell, or the calyx and stem of a flower are the most obvious of prototypes for a wide variety of drinking vessels. Within the history of these vessels a symphony of variations has been created from basic shapes, and virtually every material susceptible to manipulation by hand or tool has been called into service. An incredible number of drinking vessels have been created specifically for the consumption of wine, ranging from the silver beakers and cups of the ancient world to the brilliant blown glass of the seventeenth and eighteenth centuries and even to the disposable plastic cups of today. These display few innovations in their basic forms but virtually unlimited variations in their ornamentation.

The ritual nature of wine in the ancient world helped to determine the range of design possibilities for wine vessels, and most of the ancestors of later shapes were established early in wine history. Tradition, more than ritual, has maintained and preserved many of these shapes into our own time. The position of status and power accorded wine in the early centuries of viticulture, and to those special few entitled to possess and use the drink, laid stress on the type and decoration of the vessels from which the drink was to be consumed; design for a wine vessel had to be as significant as the precious fluid inside.

A catalogue of wine-drinking vessels would necessarily include many strange and unexpected shapes, from silver-mounted horns and animal-shaped rhytons to prized shells and even simulated shoes. However, the history of shapes can also be seen to depend primarily from two major forms – the beaker and the goblet. Both forms appeared early in the history of wine, although the beaker (and its close relative, the bowl) is possibly the earliest shape to emerge. With its flattened base and cylindrical shape – probably inspired by a truncated section of an animal's horn – the beaker requires direct contact between hand and vessel, and hence with the contents. It is a more "earth-bound" form than the goblet, in which the wine or other liquid is elevated and thus can be handled in a manner that isolates the hand from the bowl and its contents. Each form,

Beaker
1725–40
George Hanners (c. 1696–1740)
Boston, Massachusetts
Silver, 15 × 10.8
Museum of Fine Arts, Boston.
Gift of the Congregational
Church of Greenland, New
Hampshire

Beaker
1st century
Sidon, Syria, Roman period
Glass, 6.2 × 7.7
Cinzano Collection (U.K.) Ltd.

109

Lotus-shaped cup
Dynasty XVIII–XIX, 16th–13th
century B.C.
Egypt
Ceramic frit (faience), 8 × 5
Cooper-Hewitt Museum, New
York. Purchased in memory of
the Misses Hewitt, 1960-29-1

Kylix
Shallow two-handled cup
6th century B.C.
Greece
Pottery, black-figured decora-
tion, 13.6 × 32.5
Cooper-Hewitt Museum, New
York. Anonymous gift, 1921-1-1

The *kylix* was a popular drinking vessel in ancient Greece, its
capacious bowl supported on a
slender stem and elegant foot.
This *kylix* is decorated with figures that include youths with
spears and a central figure of Dionysus, holding a horn-shaped
drinking vessel.

beaker and goblet, has a strong psychological as well as visual impact,
and each has enjoyed a special line of descent into the present day.

Although the beaker was not used exclusively for wine in the ancient
world – it also held beer, which was among the earliest of man's con-
cocted intoxicants and played an important role in ancient ritual and
social usage – it appears in many wine-related contexts, in both Greece
and Rome, and in a variety of materials including silver, gold, ceramics,
and glass. Although the beaker was superseded in ritual importance by
the stemmed goblet, it has remained a vital link between the millenniums.
The form was popularized as the *Krautstrunk* in Germany during the
Middle Ages, as the tumbler cup in the seventeenth and eighteenth centuries, as the heavy cut-glass or enameled beaker in the nineteenth century, and as the everyday drinking glass in countless cafés and bistros
throughout the world today. Sturdy and stable (and often stackable in its
modern variant), the beaker had become the drinking vessel of the aver-
age person by the Middle Ages, and it has kept its "earthy" and informal
character right up to the present. This fact may help to explain the pref-
erential treatment given the beaker in religious rituals of the Protestant
church; not only did the form represent a visual and symbolic tradition,
it also reaffirmed the popular appeal and symbolic potential of an everyday object.

It is interesting to note that it was an ordinary straight-sided glass
beaker that served as the model of the wine cup in the *Last Supper* fresco
painted by the workshop of Pietro Lorenzetti in the lower basilica of San
Francesco of Assisi in the middle decades of the fourteenth century. In
choosing the beaker over the stemmed and footed chalice, a familiar element of the Mass of that time, the artist has made a subtle theological
point about the origins of the ceremony of the ritual meal, relating the
mystical event to its earthly setting.

A different but related development can be followed in the second of
the major forms for wine-drinking vessels – the goblet. The origins of a
drinking vessel raised on a stem can be traced at least as far back as the
middle of the second millennium B.C. in Egypt. Small stemmed cups,
fashioned of brilliant turquoise faience, were in use by the Eighteenth
Dynasty (1546-1336 B.C.), their shapes echoing the graceful curve of the
sacred lotus bud or blossom.

Stemmed cups of widely varying shapes proliferated in Greece, where
two-handled versions of the goblet, often with elaborate painted decoration, were produced in the form of the *kantharos* and *kylix*. These
goblets, whether ceramic or silver, functioned in ritual and ceremonial

Design for a Double Cup
Probably from *Allerley gebuntz-
wierte Fisierungen*
Published in Ansbach, 1581
Bernhard Zan (active last
quarter 16th century)
Nuremberg, Germany
Punch engraving, with hand col-
oring, 24.5 × 11.9
Cooper-Hewitt Museum, New
York. Purchased in memory of
Annie Schermerhorn Kane,
1945-17-3(1)

Double cups were a popular
form of drinking vessel in the
sixteenth century.

settings that included libations to the gods and heroes. Being the more common and available, the ceramic versions were used as everyday utensils as well as for special occasions. Ceramic and silver goblets produced in Greece served as models for many of the drinking vessels of the Romans, and by way of the Empire, the shapes were transmitted over a wide area. Silver held pride of place along with gold, as would be expected.

By the first century A.D. a new development in the technique of glass-making was to revolutionize the history of drinking vessels in general. The Romans exploited the potential of blown glass, permitting the mass production of vessels for both the serving and imbibing of wine. Many glass drinking vessels used by the Romans were of the simple bowl and beaker variety, but by the second century A.D. stemmed goblets of blown glass were being produced. Although Roman glass was not entirely clear due to trace coloration in its metal, it was the first readily available and easily worked material that permitted wine to be enjoyed visually in the vessel. From this point in time, the history of wine-drinking changed dramatically; glass-making became a sister art to wine-making.

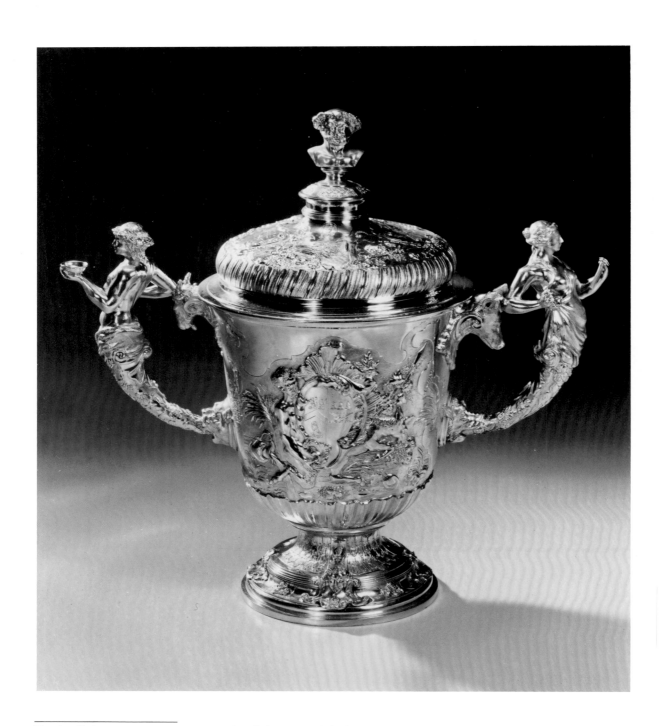

Two-handled cup
1740
William Kidney (active c. 1733)
London, England
Silver-gilt, height 37
The Worshipful Company of
Goldsmiths, London

Two-handled ceremonial drinking cups were made in large
numbers in the eighteenth century, both for use at group ceremonial occasions and for
display. The form was given an
extended life through its adop-
tion for the shape of the sporting
trophy. This cup is ornamented
with cast handles in the form of
male and female followers of
Bacchus, while the finial takes
the form of a bust of Silenus.

Goblet
1630
Venice, Italy
Blown glass, height 17
Cinzano Collection (U.K.) Ltd.

Glassware: "CIGAHotels"
Designed 1979
Lella & Massimo Vignelli and
David Law; Vignelli Designs
Manufactured by Venini
Venice, Italy
Glass, heights 11.1–15.4
Cooper-Hewitt Museum, New
York. Gift of Vignelli Associates

Wineglasses: "Capriole"
1984
Designed by Michael Boehm;
Rosenthal Glas
Germany
Glass, height 35
Courtesy Rosenthal Glas

The symbolic status of silver and gold in the ancient world, however, continued to have a dramatic effect on the history of the goblet. One need only consider the number of chalices that appeared in ecclesiastical settings from the early Christian period onward to recognize that both the precious material and the elevated form of the goblet had deep religious significance. The ritual of Communion perpetuated the chalice form, and clearly linked the ceremony to some of the oldest and most sacred uses of the wine vessel.

Tradition and ritual go hand in hand, and the course of development of the goblet into an object of special status can be traced in the history of secular ceremony. The standing cup of the Middle Ages and the Renaissance is a clear derivative of the ancient ceremonial cup, the ritual reinforcing the status of the owner and user of such a cup. The cup of power, rather than religion, forms its own chapter in the history of the goblet, with many tributary lines of development in the fraternal drinking cup, the loving cup, and the ceremonial two-handled cup, so popular

Wineglass
Late 17th–early 18th century
Flanders
Glass, height 18.3
Cinzano Collection (U.K.) Ltd.

**Set of wine glasses:
"Sommeliers"**
Designed 1976
Professor Claus Joseph Riedel;
Riedel Crystal of America, Inc.
Bohemia, New York
Glass, heights 15.2–26.7
Cooper-Hewitt Museum, New
York. Gift of Riedel Crystal of
America, Inc.

in eighteenth-century silver (which was transformed into the sports trophy).

The phenomenal success of the Venetian master glassmakers centered in Murano assured the rapid and international triumph of glass as a medium for wine-drinking. Venetian glass produced from the fourteenth century onward set a new standard of elegance and refinement in the world of wine-drinking, combining the finest talents of the glassblower and designer. Venetian glasses of the sixteenth century emphasize the fragility of the material. Their clarity and transparency allowed the color of the wine to be fully appreciated; one cannot help wondering how closely the growing dominance of glass for wine-drinking may be related to the refinement and clarification of wine itself.

By the seventeenth century, Venetian glass was being copied in glasshouses throughout Europe, with particularly noteworthy masterpieces of the glassmaker's art emanating from the workshops of the Flemish. The style became known as "façon de Venise," or in the Venetian manner. These workshops turned out broad-bowled goblets and tazzas in large numbers, and they also produced tall and elegant flutes. This exaggerated form of goblet often contrasted the elongated tapered body with an elaborately ornamented stem.

In the latter half of the seventeenth century another innovation – this time from England – contributed to the overwhelming acceptance of glass as the preferred material from which to enjoy wine. This was Ravenscroft's lead glass, which supplanted Venetian soda glass in popularity,

Goblet
c. 1762
Decorated by William Beilby, Jr. (1740–1819)
England
Glass, enamel decoration, height 21.2
Cinzano Collection (U.K.) Ltd.

This rare goblet is decorated with the arms of King George III, within scrollwork. The reverse side bears the feathers of the Prince of Wales. The goblet was made to commemorate the birth of George III's eldest son, the future King George IV.

Goblets: "Calice"
1983
Achille Castiglioni; Produzione
Danese
Milan, Italy
Glass, 20 × 8
Courtesy Produzione Danese,
Milan

Crystal champagne goblet group
Fritz Dreisbach (b. 1941)
United States
Glass, height 20.3
Courtesy Rosanne Raab Associ-
ates, Scarsdale, New York

Double wineglasses
c. 1910–20
Possibly Austria
Glass, 22.6 × 9.9
Cooper-Hewitt Museum, New
York. Gift of Mr. and Mrs.
Arthur Wiesenberger,
1967-66-19

**View of Berncastel on the
Moselle River**
From Daniel Meisner, *Thesaurus
Philo-Politicus*
1624–26
Frankfurt, Germany
Engraving, 7.6 × 14.6
The Seagram Museum, Water-
loo, Ontario

primarily due to the fact that the addition of lead to the melted silica insured the purest and most transparent material, far superior in its purity and hardness to anything that had existed previously. Besides being an ideal medium for blowing, lead glass was highly adaptable and responsive to the cutter's wheel.

By the eighteenth century, refinements in blowing techniques and the emergence of enormous glasshouses enabled the production of untold thousands of wineglasses, and with increased availability came a concurrent reduction in price. It is often hard to remember that before this the purchase of a single wineglass was a considerable investment; we have become entirely accustomed to the set of six or eight glasses as a "basic" requirement for our table. It was also in the eighteenth century that the "set" of matched glasses for table use became *de rigueur*. By the nineteenth century, the set became accessible to the multitudes as well as the elite; the next new fashion called for specific glasses for specific wines, crowding out the all-purpose wineglasses of only a few decades earlier.

The question of form and function in wineglass design is one that continues to fascinate wine connoisseurs as well as designers. Today it is not unusual to think in terms of specific shapes that are reserved for use with a specific variety of wine, and there has been an effort to back up this distinction between glass types with scientific research into the physical requirements of different wines that may help to determine the ideal shapes for their enjoyment. Certainly it is true that Ravenscroft in England in 1677 offered a variety of glasses for various wines such as

Flute glass: "Sherry Netherlands"
1984
Matteo Thun
Italy
Glass, height 23
Courtesy Matteo Thun

Tazza
c. second half 16th century
Probably Venice, or "façon de
Venise"
Glass, pattern-molded and
gilded, height 16.7
The Corning Museum of Glass,
Corning, New York

Tazza
One of a pair
1582
Maker's mark: WH
London, England
Silver-gilt, 13 × 17.2
Museum of Fine Arts, Boston.
Gift of Mr. and Mrs. Winston
F. C. Guest

"Clarrett, Sacke and Brandy." The key to the distinction seems to be rather closely related to the capacity of the vessel; whereas a claret glass was recorded as containing five ounces, that for brandy held only two. Size distinctions continue to play an important role in wineglass design.

In the unceasing process of variation that the wineglass has undergone over the course of the past two centuries, most changes have been ornamental rather than basic. With the rise in production and availability of table glass since the eighteenth century, the wineglass has been "democratized" to a degree that would have astonished our forebears.

One other footnote to the history of shapes should be included in this brief overview of the wineglass, and that involves the distinctive (and hotly debated) preferred forms for the Champagne glass. Throughout the eighteenth century, the flute-type glass was used for Champagne, as well as, presumably, for other wines. In the nineteenth century, the flat saucer-shaped "coupe" gained prominence as the standard Champagne glass. Most often a highly doubtful legend about the origin of the form is called upon to explain the emergence of this shape: that a mold taken from the breast of Marie Antoinette provided the prototype for this graceful saucer shape. Not only does this seem out of keeping with the queen's deportment, but it seems that the saucer-shaped glass was not advertised in any glass catalogues until the 1830s, long after the lovely lady was in any position to defend her modesty. In reviewing the history of the wineglass, the most obvious predecessors to the Champagne saucer are to be found in the silver tazzas of the Renaissance and in the flat tazza-shaped drinking glasses produced in Venice in the sixteenth century. Coming when it did in the nineteenth century, might not the Champagne *coupe* suggest yet another form inspired by the revival of interest in the Renaissance, and ultimately in the historicizing revival styles of the last century?

The history of wine as reflected in the myriad of designs that have accompanied its triumphal progress over the centuries and across continents can only but enrich our experience of this magical liquid. To return to Euripides, we can all agree that "if there is no god of wine, there is no love, no Aphrodite either, nor other pleasure left to man." Our celebrations and our ceremonies are given meaning through wine, and our rituals made tangible through design.

Bacchus
c. 1750
Jeremias Gottlob Rugendas
(d. 1772), after Daniel Herz the
Younger (1693–1754)
Augsburg, Germany
Engraving, 20.1 × 31.5
Cooper-Hewitt Museum, New
York. Friends of the Museum
Fund, 1938-88-8609

Suggestions for Further Reading

General History

Allen, H. Warner. *A History of Wine*. London: Faber and Faber, 1961.

Amerine, Maynard A.; Berg, Harold W.; and Cruess, William V. *The Technology of Wine Making*. 3rd ed. Westport, Conn.: The Avi Publishing Co. Inc., 1972.

Amerine, Maynard A., and Joslyn, M. A. *Table Wines: The Technology of Their Production*. 2nd ed. Berkeley: University of California Press, 1970.

Amerine, Maynard A., and Roessler, E. B. *Wines: Their Sensory Evaluation*. San Francisco: W. H. Freeman and Co., 1976.

Asher, Gerald. *On Wine*. New York: Random House, 1982.

Broadbent, Michael. *The Great Vintage Wine Book*. New York: Alfred A. Knopf, 1980.

Fadiman, Clifton, and Aaron, Sam. *The Joys of Wine*. New York: Harry N. Abrams, 1975.

Forbes, R. J. *Short History of the Art of Distillation*. Leiden, The Netherlands: 1948.

Johnson, Hugh. *Modern Encyclopedia of Wine*. New York: Simon & Schuster, 1983.

————. *Wine*. New York: Simon & Schuster, Rev. 1975.

————. *Wine Atlas of the World*. 3rd ed., rev. New York: Simon & Schuster, 1985.

Lichine, Alexis. *New Encyclopedia of Wines & Spirits*. New York: Alfred A. Knopf, 1984.

Lucia, Salvatore P. *A History of Wine as Therapy*. Philadelphia and Montreal: 1963.

————. *Wine as Food and Medicine*. New York and Toronto: 1954.

Schoonmaker, Frank. *Frank Schoonmaker's Encyclopedia of Wine*. Revised by Julius Wile. New York: Hastings House, 1978.

Sichel, Allan. *The Penguin Book of Wine*. London: Penguin Books, 1971.

Simon, André L. *Bottlescrew Days*. London: 1926.

————. *Bibliotheca Bacchica*. London: 1927. Reprinted London: Holland Press, 1972.

————. *Bibliotheca Vinaria*. London: Grant Richards Ltd., 1913.

Sutcliffe, Serena, ed. *André Simon's Wines of the World*. 2nd ed., rev. New York: McGraw-Hill, 1981.

Time-Life Books, eds. *Wine*. Alexandria, Va.: Time-Life Books, 1982.

Regional Types

Adams, Leon D. *The Wines of America*. 3rd ed., rev. New York: 1985.

Anderson, Burton. *Vino*. Boston and Toronto: Atlantic Monthly Press, 1980.

Dion, Roger. *Histoire de la Vigne et du Vin de France*. Paris: 1959.

Halasz, Zoltan. *The Book of Hungarian Wine*. Budapest: Corvino Kiado, 1981.

Hanson, Anthony. *Burgundy*. London: Faber and Faber, 1982.

Hazan, Victor. *Italian Wines*. New York: Alfred A. Knopf, 1982.

Jeffs, Julian. *The Wines of Europe*. London: Faber and Faber, 1971.

Lichine, Alexis. *Alexis Lichine's Guide to the Wines and the Vineyards of France*. Rev. ed. New York: Alfred A. Knopf, 1982.

Livingstone-Learmonth, John, and Master, Melvyn Charles. *The Wines of the Rhone*. London: Faber and Faber, 1983.

Penning-Rowsell, Edmund. *The Wines of Bordeaux*. New York: Scribner's, 1981.

Read, Jan. *The Wines of Portugal*. London: Faber and Faber, 1983.

————. *The Wines of Spain*. London: Faber and Faber, 1983.

Schoonmaker, Frank. *The Wines of Germany*. Revised by Peter M. F. Sichel. London: Faber and Faber, 1983.

Thompson, Robert, and Johnson, Hugh. *The California Wine Book*. New York: William Morrow & Co., 1976.

Wine Types

Bonal, François. *Le Livre d'Or du Champagne*. Lausanne: Editions du Grand-Pont, 1984.

Bradford, Sarah. *Port: The Englishman's Wine*. London: Christie's Wine Publications, 1978.

Cossart, Noel. *Madeira, the Island Vineyard*. London: Christie's Wine Publications, 1984.

Croft-Cooke, Rupert. *Madeira*. London: Putnam & Co., 1966.

————. *Port*. London: Putnam & Co., 1957.

————. *Sherry*. New York: Alfred A. Knopf, 1956.

Fletcher, Wyndham. *Port*. London: Sotheby Parke Bernet, 1978.

Forbes, Patrick. *Champagne: The Wine, the Land, and the People*. New York: Reynal, 1968.

Gonzalez Gordon, Manuel M. *Sherry: The Noble Wine*. London: Cassell Ltd., 1972.

Ray, Cyril. *Cognac*. London: Peter Davies Ltd., 1973.

Robertson, George. *Port*. London: Faber and Faber, 1978.

Spencer, Herbert. *Cognac Country: The Hennessy Book of a People and Their Spirit*. London: Quiller Press in association with Christie's Wine Publications, 1983.

Social and Cultural History

Bespaloff, Alexis. *The Fireside Book of Wine*. New York: Simon & Schuster, 1977.

Centre International de Liaison des Organismes de Propagande en Faveur des Produits de la Vigne (C.I.L.O.P.). *Vin et Civilisation/Vino e Civilta*. Paris: Club des Arts et Métiers, 1983; Turin: Fondazione Giovanni Dalmasso, 1983.

Chayette, Hervé. *Le Vin à Travers la Peinture*. Paris: ACR Edition Internationale, 1984.

Hale, William Harlan, and the editors of Horizon Magazine. *The Horizon Cookbook and Illustrated History of Eating and Drinking Through the Ages*. New York: American Heritage Publishing Co., Inc., 1968.

Hyams, Edward. *Dionysus: A Social History of the Wine Vine*. London: Thames and Hudson, 1965.

Lamb, R. B., and Mittelberger, C. G. *In Celebration of Wine and Life*. San Francisco: The Wine Appreciation Guild, 1980.

Saintsbury, George. *Notes on a Cellar-Book*. Rev. ed. New York: Mayflower Books, 1978.

Seltman, C. *Wine in the Ancient World*. London: Routledge & Kegan Paul, 1957.

Simon, André L. *The History of the Wine Trade in England*. 3 vols. London: 1906–9. Reprinted London: The Holland Press, 1964.

Weinhold, Rudolf. *Vivat Bacchus: A History of the Vine and Its Wine*. Trans. Neil Jones. Hertfordshire, England: Argus Books, Ltd., 1978.

Woschek, Heinz-Gert. *Der Wein: Geschichte und Geschichten über Jahrtausende Bilder und Dokumente*. Munich: Callwey, 1971.

Younger, William. *Gods, Men, and Wine*. Cleveland, Ohio: The Wine and Food Society in association with World Publishing Company, 1966.

Catalogues of Exhibitions and Collections

Exposition Rétrospective de la Vigne et le Vin dans l'Art. Paris: Musée des Arts Décoratifs, Pavillon de Marsan, Palais du Louvre, May–July, 1936.

The Goldsmith & the Grape: Silver in the Service of Wine. London: A Goldsmiths' Company Exhibition, Goldsmiths' Hall, 11–28 July 1983.

Lagrange, André. *Catalogue: Musée du Vin de Bourgogne à Beaune*. Paris: Editions G. P. Maisonneuve et Larose, 1966.

Le Vin de France dans l'Histoire. Paris: Hôtel de Rohan, April 16–May 26, 1953.

Special Subjects

Anex, Paul; Champ, André; Sauter, Pierre; et. al. *Arts et Métiers du Vin*. Musée Vaudois de la Vigne et du Vin, Château d'Aigle. Denges-Lausanne: Editions du Verseau, 1979.

Dumbrell, Roger. *Understanding Antique Wine Bottles*. Suffolk, England: Antique Collectors Club, 1983.

Kilby, Kenneth. *The Cooper and His Trade*. London: John Barker, 1971.

Logoz, Michel. *Wine Label Design*. New York: Rizzoli, 1984.

Mazenot, R. *Les Tastevins à Travers les Siècles*. Grenoble, France: 1977.

Penzer, N. M.. *The Book of the Wine Label*. London: Home and Van Thal, 1947.

Taransaud, Jean. *Le Livre de la Tonnellerie*. Paris: La Roue à Livres Diffusion, 1976.

Watney, Bernard M., and Babbidge, Homer D. *Corkscrews for Collectors*. London and New York: Sotheby Parke Bernet, 1981.